LOST DISCUSSIONS

LOST DISCUSSIONS

KAUSHIK BANERJEE

ADROIT

Adroit Publishers
New Delhi

ISBN : 978-81-87393-26-9

First Published in 2015

Published by

ADROIT PUBLISHERS

4675/21, Ganpati Bhawan, Ansari Road,
Daryaganj, New Delhi-110 002

Phone : 011-23266030

Distributors

AKHIL BOOK DISTRIBUTORS

email: akhilbooks@yahoo.com
akhilbks@gmail.com

Cover page by Design Print

*Typesetting—**Kumud Printographics**, Delhi-110053*

E-mail: vedkumud123@gmail.com

Printed at: Milan Printers, New Delhi

"This book is dedicated to

my wife

Jhumi

my Princess

Isheeta

and

my son

Ishaan Banerjee"

" Thank you

Prosenjit Mukherjee!

For weaving many
stories together,
you are a great friend"

ABOUT THE AUTHOR

"I don't exactly remember my first meeting with Kaushik. I don't blame my grey cells as I think it is quite obvious for anyone to forget this first meeting if it happens in a class of 30 – 40 children all shouting, crying inconsolably and running towards the door to get out of the room. This was the first day in kindergarten for both of us.

While I took my routine work too seriously at school, he spent all his energy in being creative and bringing out innovative ideas sitting on the last bench of the class, lost in his own world, often careless and relaxed. I have always known him as a "Down to Earth" personality. A practical person with strong reason and big ambitions, still attached to his roots.

My first experience of reading him was a poem called "My Opinion on Him". In simple words, this poem presents beautifully the feelings of a son after getting his exam results, which any one can connect or relate to easily. Even now, this is very prominent in his writings. He has a unique capacity of being able to pick up or select mundane aspects of life and depict them differently in a thought-provoking way.

Lost Discussions is Kaushik's second publication after the great success of *Zero After Nine* where his work has been appreciated and well-received. The accent of a poet has changed from monosyllables to long narrations. Change is what is obvious and change in his mode of deciphering was about to come. Every story is like a slice of life itself, realisations are far from mundane. This is what he has poignantly incorporated. The discussions are not consummate, but of course they are alive. Had I been the author, I would have named them "Half Discussions".

Sushil Agarwal

CONTENTS...

One

THREE **F**ATHERS—'I have something to discuss with you. Can we meet at the bar in Marine Drive?' Anshu sounded anxious over the phone as he spoke to Sachin. 'OK.

Govind is also in Mumbai. Let's all meet tonight,' replied Sachin.

Anshu, Govind and Sachin were childhood friends. Anshu had settled in Delhi after his father told him to take charge of the northern zone of the family business. He frequently visited Mumbai to learn business tactics from his father. He was unmarried. Govind, who was married for four years, had business in Surat. He often came to Mumbai to meet his parents. Sachin worked for a nationalised bank and was married for couple of years now.

In the evening, Sachin and Govind were the first ones to reach the bar. They ordered food and drinks and started chatting. It was like the old times. Govind put one arm around Sachin's shoulders and said, 'So, how is life going? Busy funding corporates? How is your wife?'

'Oh! She is fine though a bit bored and lonely. I remain busy the entire day and reach home in the evening around 8,' Sachin sounded concerned. 'She has told me too many times to shift close to my office in Prabhadevi. But you know how it is in banks. They provide accommodation as per availability and grades. I keep telling her to be patient. She is a teacher. I tell her to keep teaching. But then, life is not always the way we want it to be.'

Govind smiled at Sachin and said, 'You are better off, brother. My wife is a homemaker. She is always at home and equally demanding when it comes to me. She calls me up every day in office and asks me to come home early. I can understand her loneliness.'

When Anshu entered the bar, the two had already finished one drink. He ordered another round and said, 'What's the discussion about? Wives or girlfriends?'

'We're not as lucky as you are. We are talking about our wives' loneliness,' said Govind. 'It's so absurd when my wife starts fighting with me without reason. These unnecessary wrangles are just too much for me now.'

Govind always envied Anshu's happy-go-lucky attitude. Anshu always had enough money to be extravagant. Govind thought he was lucky.

To change the mood, Anshu narrated an incident. 'Once, when one of my key managerial staff, a decent B-school grad, joined my company, I asked him if he had children. He said he had one. So I advised him to have one more. When he looked at me flustered, I told him that the wife would remain busy with the children and he would be able to focus on work,' he laughed as others joined him.

Then Anshu continued, 'Hey what's wrong with you guys? Why have both of you not moved on with life? Why don't either of you have a child? I did not marry, but even I am thinking of having a child.'

As both looked at him in confusion, Anshu said, 'I had called to discuss this. I want to adopt a child.'

Govind responded rather sharply, 'How can you adopt a child when you are not even married? You want to leave business and become a baby-sitter?'

Still laughing, Anshu said, 'Then you guys give me a child, yaar.' He, then, added, 'I have decided to adopt a child and that's it.'

Anshu's outburst left both dazed and thoughtful. Govind slowly started talking about his problem. 'My wife longs for a child. I, too, want to have children. But doctors say there are medical complications. There is some problem with me because of which we cannot have children. We have been disturbed about this for quite some time now,' as Anshu kept a comforting hand on his, Govind continued, 'I don't want to go for IVF, IUV or have a test-tube baby. I know that the woman can develop complications. Every week or fortnight she would need injections. Also, these are long procedures. I may not be fully informed about these, but I do not want my wife to go through physical and mental trauma.' At the end when nothing happens it is far more disturbing.

Sachin nodded in agreement and said, 'I have a different problem. My wife is a working woman. She thinks she can manage home and work together. Doctors have said that both of us are medically fit. But somehow, my wife has not been able to conceive.'

'I don't want to get married,' said Anshu. 'But I really want a child.'

'So how will you keep the child? Where will the child stay and who will take care of the child's necessities?' asked Govind.

'I think I could adopt a child from an orphanage. I will pay for all the expenses—food, studies, medicines, clothes etc. This morning someone came to my house and explained the model of his orphanage. It's quite different from the others. It finds people who can fund children. It also finds people who want to raise them as their own children. So an orphan can get a home as well as money. It suits my kind of people, who have the money but not the means to raise children,' said Anshu.

'It's a great idea, Anshu. You know what? My wife and I have also decided to adopt a girl. We think it is better than going through repeated medical procedures. It would also make us feel good. My wife says that in Mumbai, orphanages allow you to pick children whose features, skin colour, hair etc match yours,' said Govind excitedly.

'It's nice that you, too, are thinking of doing something so noble. As for me, I will need more time to take the plunge,' said Sachin. Just then his phone rang. 'It's my wife,' he smiled, 'she wants me to be home for dinner.'

It was late. Everyone headed for their homes thinking what life held for them.

Seven years passed. The three friends never met or spoke to each other—blame it on time or circumstances.

So when Sachin got a phone call from Anshu, he was elated. Sachin had many stories to tell Anshu. The first thing he blurted out was that his wife had finally given birth to a child. They had a son and had named him Rahul. Govind had shifted to Mumbai. It was his daughter's birthday today and the family was invited home for the party. 'You come over too. Govind will be so happy to see you,' Sachin said.

'Yes, I will. How old is Govind's child?'

'She is eight.' Anshu quickly went to the toy shop from where he used to buy toys for the girl he had adopted. In all these years, he had learnt how to buy toys for children. Not just his own child, but people of his age also had children for whom he would buy toys. He had attended more birthday parties than beer parties by now. That was not because he was drinking less. It was because his friends were drinking less. He was unmarried, lonely and had turned into a drunkard. His father had died. His mother lived alone in Mumbai and he lived alone in Delhi.

Anshu knew that children's birthday parties would have animated games and the cake-cutting ceremony. He hated all this now. To avoid these, he deliberately reached Govind's house late.

Govind hugged Anshu. Seeing him, Govind was happy and aghast at the same time.

'Whatever happened to you, yaar? You look much

older than your age,' Sachin seemed concerned. Anshu had lost all his hair, had put on weight and had a big moustache. The ever-present smile had disappeared. Anshu just smiled indifferently.

The party was in full swing. Loud music played as children hysterically ran about the house. Chips, cold drinks, chocolate wrappers and balloons could be seen in every corner of the house. He could see Govind's daughter enjoying herself, too. She looked so much like Govind's wife.

Anshu talked very little now. His two friends felt sad for him. Both were trying to keep control over their excited children, but would find time to sit with him at short intervals and chat. Their wives, too, would come and try to make him feel at home. It was 11.30 pm when the party broke up. All the parents had taken their children home. Knowing Anshu, Sachin asked Govind to get some beer. The threesome was together again. At last, Anshu felt at home.

Govind and Sachin started discussing how their lives had changed after becoming parents. More often than not they were running errands for children. That was the most important though most enjoyable thing. They discussed children's education, their circle of friends. None, however, started the uncomfortable topic of adoption. He wanted to tell Govind that his daughter looked quite a lot like his wife, but refrained. 'It may turn the conversation bitter,' he thought. The air-conditioner was running at full blast, but Anshu was sweating. There was something nagging him.

After about an hour, Anshu stood up to leave. 'Let me drop you,' said Sachin and picked up the car keys. The two wives were too tired so it was agreed that Sachin and his wife would spend the night at Govind's house.

Soon, Anshu and Sachin were on the road. 'Buy me a bottle of beer, Sachin,' Anshu said. As Sachin drove, Anshu took a swig from the can and asked, 'From which orphanage did Govind take his child?'

'I don't know the name. It is somewhere in Mulund.'

Anshu probed further, 'Have you seen it? Is it near the church at Mulund?'

'Bang on! That's the place. You seem to know a lot about orphanages. You, too, adopted a child, didn't you?'

'Yes, after our last meeting, I went to this orphanage at Mulund. The management showed me all kinds of children. Some were blind, some physically challenged, and some were spastic. But I was enamoured by a small girl who was new to the orphanage. She looked very sweet, but was crying so much. The more I went close to her, the louder she would cry. I told the management that I would pay all the expenses for this child. They agreed.

'A few years ago when I went to meet her, she ran towards me and gave me a very warm hug. The other children were jealous of her. I heard a 14-year-old grumbling that if I had so much money, why could I not pay for all of them? I felt so bad that day that I promised myself never to go to that orphanage again, though I doubled the donation amount.

'I think the girl Govind has adopted is the same girl. She could not recognise me perhaps because she had seen me properly just once and was busy celebrating her birthday. Thanks to Govind and his wife, she has found a home. I am really pained to think what must have happened to the rest in the orphanage,' Anshu looked extremely sad.

'Brother, even I feel like helping them,' said Sachin, 'but we cannot do everything for everyone. I have been thinking about this for some time and penned it down.'

Anshu's face lit up suddenly. 'Oh! You had a habit of writing. I would be glad to hear something from you again after so many years.'

Sachin started—

'I wanted to be in philanthropy,
Saw opportunities, I could not grab.
My worries kept me living,
Ended up, being a hermit crab.

Now lost dreams, sail my vision,
Forgotten relationships blink.
Ends now don't have a reason,
Broken years do not link.

My stories have lost meaning now,
I am ashamed to share them.
A corner to begin yet again! I seek,
But fate and it's mayhem.

I wanted to be in philanthropy
But the world is too sane.'

Two

THE MIRROR—Whenever I entered the office, every day I used to see this guard who made faces at me!

I knew he was afraid of me, but still he dares to look at me with an elfish grin? I hated his eyes; they looked at me with indifference, as if they understand what I am thinking of... I know he can't be a cause of any harm to me, I know the moment he opens his mouth, how I can make his life difficult. But ignoring and being indifferent are two different things. While ignoring you make people believe that you don't care what they are feeling. In being indifferent, one makes sure that even if they are aware of the apparent danger, they kind of don't care about it.

Now this lady Sneha, she somehow is not able to make it to the office ever in time. While she walks in, she makes sure to say good morning and looks at her watch. I get pride to know that I reach office before her. This gives me pleasure, so what if I am the boss! Why can't I come earlier? And if I can, why can't others do the same?

I found Sneha a very sweet looking lady when she was recruited for the position of head analytics. Now she kind of takes too much of my data and time. Ah! Like everyone, she has to impress the MD.

But I know my work best, today late evening we have this review, and I shall show my wits as well as my work. Mr. More, the MD will reach at 5 p.m. The review starts at 6.30 p.m. My belief used to be

When boss is in town...

Don't be smart, neither react!

Whatever they like and don't,

Invariably, please do act!

Do your job, and do it well...

There is no room for curiosity,

Dumb, old and cribbing people

Don't have space in my city!

Their whims can keep families awake,

Their fancies may make you spend...

I could see that today people are less confident, since they have to sit late today! Ha ha ha...I laugh at their misery. The incomparable wish! To go back home, and run away from work. Men and women, useless crap! And the money they take is like uuuufff...but all these people are capable of doing, not good, but bad things! They all know how to waste more money, more time, sit idle and gossip...God knows where these people will go?

I am doing business for them. I am making the money for the company which translates into their salaries. These people will never grow in this organisation! My suspicion for them is not about myself, but for the harm they are capable of inflicting on the company's performance!

I don't understand when I can sell such a product, why on earth do we need all these people? Service, after sales, billing could very well be done with fewer people. Why so many people? Give me more people; I am more than able to do more business... Mr. More will be happy to see these numbers, these are my numbers.

It was already 12.30, by the time I could close my presentation, which would get discussed this evening. While I finished my work very soon, on my stroll within the office saw everyone working on their presentations. People who could not finish their work in the last two years, how will they finish it now? Funny thoughts kept me busy. My work is always done; the entire staff keeps creeping about it.

It is two years since I have joined as the sales head for an electronics gadget manufacturing company. The company has its head office in Ahmedabad, and my boss the MD Shashak More is also based at Ahmedabad. I am heading sales for Haryana and this is the first time I will be interacting with the MD on professional achievements.

In June the mercury rises very high in Gurgaon. The place where my office is located, the moment you move out of the AC, your skin burns. It's like you are in a steel manufacturing company and the entire city turns into a furnace! AC is the only solace. In these two years, the idea of getting married has been procrastinated. These numbers, these years, have kept me away from family. Friends meet late in the evening, since all are on their own in Gurgaon. With friends these days beer is so flat! Everybody has to flaunt their numbers, apart from Sushil.

Sushil is a nice chap, an old friend of mine; he had always been ahead in academics. Got through IIT in the first attempt, is now working for a software company for the last four years. But these IT people are so different, their virtual world is so boring... Sitting in the office for more than an hour makes my mind blow up. It's the same people around every day! While I meet new people every time I walk out.

Sushil somehow manages to find time; he always meets me with a smile on his face as if he is still in college. He is the same old guy, always cheerful. I invited him for dinner yesterday with Das, who is in my team. I somehow see no change in Sushil and this makes it more intolerable for me, I don't know what's wrong with me! Doesn't look good enough to me! I shared my feelings; he said he is not bothered! These friends do change with time. Or have I changed? God knows...

But Sneha was laughing; her lunch box has always allured my hunger. She was having lunch as usual and her nicely done boxes, colourful plastic bottle in which she carried either juices or *lassi* has always made me feel for home. The *chapattis* she carries had the hue of my mother's *rotis*.

It seems like she is done with her Goddamn 'analytics'! What information could she have got? I called up my guy based out at Karnal, his data was pending for my PPT. Just one number! But the person is like... he is always sipping on his iced tea forever on the beach. However you shake the glass the ice does not melt!

He has a strange way of talking, the accent! I detest his accent. He would always say 'you told me yesterday only' 'I am sending the mail in a moment'. I lose my temper with his attitude; somehow I have heard he always remains happy. Got to know he is generally a very helpful guy. But what data has Sneha got? The people who assist Sneha look more satisfied. I have always felt this contentment is due to the lesser job they have to do...

I could feel the eyes are all around me, as if I am taking away someone else's pie. It was apparent to me that there was suspicion about my work, my numbers. But my confidence on self and my numbers kept consoling me about the review. It's two years since I am heading sales in this office and the quest for excellence has never gone down deep within me. I am expecting a promotion in the upcoming appraisal.

In my first job, my figures in terms of professional achievements were beyond my expectations. Now was the time for rewards, recognitions and applause. My expectations from Mr More were very straight.

In my MBA days I was taught how to get my job done by others. When you can get something by carrot, use the carrot, when it's time for the stick, it's time for the stick!

But getting your work done is not that theoretical; real people are different, an ocean of their thoughts. At times you use one thing you have realized and have worked well in a situation, again at times something very stupid starts working. But it is a game; I have started playing in this first job from the last two years. I love this game now! Every day a new set of situations, a new set of people, manipulations and mind games.

While some are tired of playing this game, others enjoy playing it. Every day a new game, every night thoughts of losing and winning... This game has gone into my blood so well, that excellence is the only reflection.

It was quarter to four in the evening, when people from various locations had started to reach the regional office. Funny people, very sad people and people who have the kind of faces as if it is a crime to meet Mr. More. But Mr. More and his expectations! As high as his name. The overwhelming need for excellence, doing better, achieving more...

While most of the people were dressed well, some needed a shave, some travelling long distances, have unkempt hair. That's the reason I make sure my team is completely presentable. Everybody had to come in formals and with a tie, sleeves strictly rolled down. Some people look so funny when they get dressed properly, but Das never obeyed. He was fine professionally, did his numbers well, yet I have told him on many occasions to be more presentable. The impression I carried of him was OK looking at his numbers and to my utter surprise he accepted this as 'OK!'.

This Das was referred to me by Sushil, or else we would never have recruited him. We had good times at his place and Sushil's place many times, but Das is a loud mouth. He always says things to people directly...once he told me that in the last two years, he is seeing more scars on my face, that my teeth are getting larger, hair has grown out of my ears and stuff like that. I never found his way of talking acceptable, but he was fine professionally and in numbers.

By the time it was around five, on my own I went to the meeting room. Got the information that Mr More had reached Delhi. I called up the administration guy to make sure that everything is in place. For snacks there were sandwiches and tea. I had to count people who are attending this meeting, vegetarians/non-vegetarians; some were for coffee, some for soft drinks. Made sure the same was in place and altered the existing arrangements.

I made sure that the chairs are placed in the proper manner; I called up the guy in Karnal now and actually had to shout at him at the top of my voice for the data I was waiting for. As usual he was smiling on the other side of the phone as if knowing what was coming. He said he had already sent the information and again I had to shout at him for not informing me. His casual attitude, has always given my temper a ride.

I rushed for my desk and laptop, I could again see people are very busy now. My confidence started picking up again. I have done so much, already informed the office administration to update Mr More on my additions in the overall arrangement. Data had come and my PPT was done. I wanted to check it on the projector in the meeting room, the fonts, the background and all.

In no time I reached the meeting room, connected my laptop to the projector and it was not working! I was the first who had to discuss the presentation; I soon called up the IT guy in the office. This person has always helped me, in odd hours; he would always take my calls. Be it mails not working, password reset, the VC room, etc.

He showed up soon, some connecting cable was the problem now. This guy had to get up on the meeting table and change the cable. While he was replacing the cable connected to the projector, a part of the table under him collapsed! This thin fellow fell down! And his head hit against a chair's corner. Started bleeding instantly, and I was all nerves. I remembered how my mother used to cover my face whenever she saw anyone bleeding in a traumatic situation; I covered my face with both my hands.

This huge noise made everybody run to the meeting room. Soon I realized that others have come to the room and were equally taken aback. I picked up this fellow, put his arm on my shoulder and started for the first aid box, which someone was already holding. Soon I realized it would not suffice and the bleeding had not stopped, I shouted for the ambulance. By this time this person was able to stand up, and said he would not need an ambulance rather a drop to the doctor would help him more.

I looked around and the scared faces of people there told me that I was the one who had to take him to the doctor. I asked a colleague to hold the guy for a while and ran for my car keys which were there on my work station. It was twenty-five passed six by the time I could come out of the doctor's cabin. The doctor assured me that it is just a bruise and would heal soon. He was able to sense the trauma I had been through and reassured me that he should be fine soon.

On my way back, feeling slightly relaxed, I switched on the radio.

There is an old mirror at home,

I took it out, uncovered it...

Imagined the faces I used make

Once upon a time, and I sit!

To realize I look like a crook!

Invited my friends they looked the same...

My boss took the shape of hound

My family! Oh I have no name...

The entire world was something else

Some cartoons, some saints and all

I kept on looking at the old mirror

Shocked like never, the faces befall!

I helped someone unknown to me

The mirror the trash was very old...

By the time I could make it back to the office it was seven thirty and to my utter relief the meeting had already started as if nothing in this world was waiting for me. Mr. More stood up and seeing him everyone else did the same. I passed on the information that the IT guy is fine now.

Sneha's PPT was on, and as it went on, it had better things on my achievements. She was able to effectively sight some of my good work which I had not known myself.

All PPTs, all data, started looking superfluous to me by now. I started with my PPT and Mr More added how I have managed things so well in this part of the country. The long standing challenges I faced every day started melting like wax. This wax candle was so small that it could not stand the entire meeting.

Mr. More took us out for dinner that night after the meeting. The IT guy had also come and he was sitting there with Das who as usual was having beer and making faces. I got to know the name of this IT guy was Vijay. Today a glass of beer made me feel good and I started sending SMS to my family and friends on jokes I receive this morning.

Three

THE SUCCESSFUL COWARD—The last I met Manoj Agarwal was eight years ago, at Ravenshaw College, Cuttack. We studied together there. Manoj was a bright student and wanted to be a doctor. His father had a big shop in a small city in Bihar and wanted Manoj to join his business. There would be a constant tussle in Manoj's mind over what he would do. While his teachers encouraged him to study medicine, his father pulled him towards family business.

He cleared the entrance exams for dental science in 2004 as well as in 2005. But his father was averse to the prospect of pursuing the career. In 2006, he finally gave up his dream of becoming a doctor. That year, the Odisha government had set up a quota for students studying from outside Odisha. Only 10 per cent seats across all faculties were open for students from other states. The level of competition was so fierce that he did not get a seat anywhere.

Manoj was left with no option but to join his father's business. None of his college friends heard from him in all these years. It was a pleasant surprise when bumped into him at a shopping mall. He recognised me before I could. I realised that it was because of my bald pate. I had very little hair even when I was in college. He was the same shy person. Both of us were soon exchanging our lives in the years that we missed.

'I am in the mining business in Odisha. What about you?'

'I shifted to Kolkata five years back and joined an automobile manufacturing company,' I said, smiling at the girl he was carrying in his arms. 'Is she your daughter?'

'Yes,' he said giving her an adoring glance.

'Oh! I would love to meet you wife,' I said.

'I did not marry,' he said.

My jaw dropped, but the expression on his face told me that any more queries on the subject would not be welcomed.

Manoj was always like that. If he did not want to share something, he would never talk about it. I thought that he had grown egocentric over the years. I invited him home, but he declined saying he did not have much time and had to return to Odisha.

'My daughter has developed a large muscle on her back. It is increasing by the week and has bulged out now. I ignored it initially, but now she complains of pain,' said Manoj. 'I have to take her to a good doctor. I came to a shopping mall to buy toys for her to keep her mind off from the pain.'

'Do you remember Sudhir? He became a doctor and is in Kolkata right now. We can meet him. It will be a good get-together and you can discuss your daughter's problem with him. He will refer you to a good doctor.'

It was agreed that both of us would meet at the same mall the next day and drive down to Sudhir's clinic.

I saw Manoj leaving in a brand new Mercedes. 'He definitely has a lot of money,' I thought. In college, Manoj never flaunted his money though his father had immense wealth from his business.

I called up Sudhir and told him about the get-together. He was more than pleased about it.

When I reached the shopping mall in a hired taxi the next day, I saw Manoj's Mercedes parked right in front of the mall. He was waiting inside the car for me. We started the journey—a 45-minutes drive.

'You wanted to join the Forces, didn't you? What was so good about the automobile company?' he asked.

'I wanted to, but then I got engrossed in studies and joined the bandwagon of students who wanted to take up engineering and other technical streams.'

'Yes, I understand. Anyway, there's not much glory in the Forces these days.' Manoj's statement just left me stumped, and I wondered if he was the same guy I had known in college.

'You see, the number of wars across the globe is decreasing. Most countries have not seen a war in decades. I definitely do not say that security is not important, but these days the Forces are improved just to show strength to the country across the border. Isn't it ridiculous the way small and developing countries spend money to buy arms? Developed nations' foreign currency soars, and people in small nations live in penury,' he said.

'Countries need to build up Forces for contingency,' I said.

'This is exactly what I want to say. If I have to join the Forces just for contingency, I would rather be a civilian and create wealth for the nation. Because at the end of the day, my wealth would add up to the country's wealth and my taxes would help improve contingency,' he said.

'And what would happen if there was a war suddenly? Can money save the country? Had it been so, why would developed countries spend so much on security? Strong Forces and a sound security make the entire nation feel safe,' I debated.

'Ha! They take money from us and spend it on buying arms. If all the countries have arms, which one would like to go to war? We spend far more than we earn from this business.'

'Everything is not business,' I protested. 'It's like toning your body, taking care of your health. One must take preventive and proactive measures.'

The debate had to stop because we had reached Sudhir's clinic. It was inside a big commercial building. Manoj looked up at the small hoardings hanging on the building's façade and saw Sudhir's. Sudhir was a heart specialist. His chamber was small but cosy. Diagrams of human organs and advertisements of medicine manufacturers hung on all the walls of the chamber. Five patients were waiting to see him. As Sudhir continued to attend to his patients, we waited to see him.

'Hey, I knew Sudhir had joined a big medical college in Delhi. Why did he return to Kolkata?' asked Manoj.

'He is still working there,' I said, 'He is on leave right now. He will return to the hospital in two years. Here, too, he is attached to a hospital.'

The hospital in Delhi was world renowned, and the one in Kolkata was quite small. Manoj knitted his brows and asked, 'Why? Does the hospital pay him more?'

'No. He said there are many BPL patients in Kolkata.'

Manoj burst out laughing, 'You mean Below Poverty Line? After studying medicine for so long, he is trying his hands on the poor? Ha, ha! Of course, they are the ones who will never complain.'

I preferred to keep quiet. When he calmed down, he said, 'This is strange. If he wanted to do charity, he could have joined a government hospital.'

Then as a sudden thought struck him, he said, 'Remember in the 1980s and 90s, doctors would go to each house to attend to patients for petty fees? Patients would get well at home and wouldn't need to go to big hospitals.'

'Doctors ask for more money now because people's earnings have increased. Can you compare what your father earned with your earnings?' said I.

'I am not worried about the money, dear,' said Manoj. 'The problem is that there are not enough doctors. The difference between the number of doctors who wanted to pursue medicine two decades ago and the number now is huge. The number of colleges that increased over the years is not proportionate to the country's population.'

The debate was turning more into Manoj's monologue.

'To add to our woes, many medical students have left our country and settled abroad. What will happen to the people of this country? Statistics show that the number of doctors per person has drastically decreased in the past four decades. We should address this issue first and then think about the nation's security.'

'Our country has high level of intellect and educational infrastructure. We can easily double the number of doctors. These doctors can help build the nation healthier.'

'But Manoj, in trying to do so, many countries have lost their standard of education,' I said.

'Trust me, no one from those countries travel out for medical reasons. They are doing absolutely fine within their geographical boundaries and do not need Indian doctors to treat them.

'All I am saying is that instead of the country paying huge bills on free medical support to the poor, medical insurance and interest/return on FDI, we should increase the number of seats in medical colleges. This will save our people.

'Today, each person I talk to, is worried about saving money. Let me ask you a simple question. How much of your savings have you kept for your family's health? How much have you kept for your children's education? If the government addresses these as issues, our lives would improve. This is when we will feel secure. While we pay

30% tax in this country and get nothing decent, developed nations pay 40% and get everything for free!'

I agreed with him but said, 'Manoj, securing the same standard of medical education across the country is asking for too much. It would require many more faculties, infrastructure and governance. At present, all that is missing.'

'So let people die,' Manoj said sarcastically. 'Some doctors make huge money from this lacuna in the system. Despite having the best quality doctors, there are so many cases of medical negligence every day. Why do we think that one medical entrance examination is so supreme, that it cannot be undone?' he said bitterly.

'Hey Manoj, still preparing for the medical entrance?' Sudhir patted Manoj's back. Both of us had been so engrossed in the debate that we did not realise that all the patients had left. Sudhir's words brought us back to reality. We hugged each other happy to meet once again.

'No, Sudhir. I want to open a hospital in a mining area in Odisha. Do you know some good doctors who would be interested to work there? They can travel once a week to that place. This way, locals will be able to avail of good medical facilities. I plan to keep some in-house doctors as well,' Manoj said.

Sudhir liked the proposition and started discussing details of the project. When Manoj raised the topic of his daughter, Sudhir enquired about his wife. 'She died six years ago during childbirth. She suffered some complications. She died due to wrong diagnosis and lack of proper care.'

Despite his problems, the confidence Manoj had in life made me think—

LOST DISCUSSIONS

This fire can never exhaust,
It is a tale of intolerant pride,
Failures in every step tumble,
Hope keeps its high ride.

Confidence, not intellect or else,
Faith and not just sanity,
Keeps rolling this heart and head,
And immeasurable vanity.

Look back at the power of truth,
Standing strong against oneself,
Found you between something,
Like existence of an elf.

The willingness to abide the mind,
And a wish to convey the heart.

Four

The Idea—Free will. That's what was most thrilling about biking. The freedom, the feeling of being alone on the road, may be with friends who let you stay alone and free, exhilarated these youngsters. Raju, Venkat, Saurabh and Kesam were best friends in high school. Their love for biking bound them together even after school. They enjoyed going to the jungles and move around among tall trees and amidst the bounties of nature. They loved to watch the clear sky, breathe in fresh air and touch the tender leaves. They would shake small trees to allow the morning dew to fall on them. The idea of watching small streams and getting enchanted by its music, listening to the birds' songs and showing them to friends, was something only bikers could understand, they thought. The dare and the challenge biking involved was most invigorating.

It was Raju's idea to go to Barog—a quaint hill station near Kasauli in Himachal Pradesh. The idea was to snatch away the weekend to do what they loved most before all got busy with work. Saurabh and Venkat had completed engineering from mediocre colleges in Delhi. They lived together in Delhi and were in search of jobs. Kesam was from Manipur. She has done MBA, not from the best colleges. She had received an offer letter from a company in Mumbai and would leave Chandigarh within a month. Raju had stayed in Chandigarh after school and graduated in commerce. He had joined his father's flourishing business of restaurants.

The friends often met during holidays and spent time together to share new ideas, dispel boredom, or just have fun. They would always take three motorcycles, and mostly rode up to the Himalayas. From Chandigarh, the hills look very close. Half-an-hour's drive would take you to Kalka, from where the Himalayas begin.

When Raju mentioned the idea, all jumped at it and were ready to brave the mid-June heat. As usual, they would leave early on Saturday morning with only a few belongings.

Raju reached the designated spot first, before the crack of dawn. Soon, Venkat and Saurabh arrived, riding on their own motorcycles. Kesam came with her boyfriend, Rohit. This time, the friends were taking four bikes up the hill.

It was almost 9.30 am. After crossing Parwanoo, they stopped at the famous Timber Trail Hotel—the place where they would take their first break. It served tea, bread and omelettes and even noodles for breakfast.

They ordered tea and noodles. This was the first time they had actually seen each other properly after a long break. Happy to see their friends, they chatted and laughed loudly. They discussed the heat. 'Yaar, Delhi is just as hot as Chandigarh,' said Saurabh. When Venkat and Saurabh together narrated how dirty their room was, everyone was in splits—not just for their stories, but also for their broken Hindi. Venkat was from Chennai and his endeavours to speak Hindi enchanted everyone. Saurabh was from Bengal and he would mix up the two genders while talking. 'Don't ever come to our room,' laughed Saurabh, 'The area under our beds is the stickiest place on earth.' The two gave a Hi-five gesture and started digging into their noodles. Rohit belonged to Manipur just like Kesam. He had a glamorous hairstyle. The couple looked sweet together. Both could barely speak Hindi. Raju had never lived anywhere apart from Chandigarh. But because of his friends he knew the vanity of a Bengali, the logic of a Tamilian and the sweetness of someone from the north-east. Language never came as a barrier for the friends. No one even cared whether what they spoke was correct or incorrect. The communication happened between hearts.

Their next stop was for lunch. It was the usual order of *chapattis* with *Dal makhani*. They knew these were the only things cooked fresh. Of course, omelettes had to come along with it.

They reached the Himachal Pradesh Tourism Development Corporation Hotel in Barog at 3 p.m. in the afternoon. They took a 15-minute break and then headed for a small river, around a kilometre from the hotel. This river was everyone's favourite place. It was absolutely quiet but for the sound of gushing water and the birds. Like most of lower Himachal, this place, too, does not have many animals apart from cows, goats and stray dogs. After dusk, they walked back to the hotel.

In the evening, they were together at the balcony of Venkat and Saurabh. Over coffee, smoked chicken and cottage cheese, Venkat initiated an idea that brought everyone into the conversation.

'I have designed a small, portable lift that can be attached to the balconies of duplex houses. This lift will be able to carry goods up to 200 kg. It would not cost more than one lakh rupees and increase the market value of houses that do not have lifts. It will be very helpful to the elderly.'

'Hey, if the design is good, you could make good money,' said Rohit. 'But all the lifts would need government agencies' approval. How will you manage that?'

'I am sure it will pass the quality check. It is just a matter of time. I will finish the design and immediately start working on the first portable lift.'

Saurabh had a different idea. 'I want to make a mobile application device that can be used in hotels and restaurants. I have heard there is a lot of pilferage in the unorganized food sector. What is your experience, Raju?'

'You are right, Saurabh,' said Raju. 'At least three people are required to monitor daily operations in my hotel, which has only 80 seats. I wonder how bigger hotels manage.'

'That's why I have decided to design an application and a gadget. The gadget will look like the dialling pad of a telephone or its touch screen. Each dish on the menu will have a specific code. The customer can feed in the code into the gadget. This will be directly displayed in the kitchen. Then, the hotel owner will only need people to deliver the order.

'After this, I want to open a company that would provide maintenance and service contracts with various small and big restaurants. I will sell the device along with all necessary software and hardware and will also do their annual maintenance.'

Venkat was not sure. 'But in India, a lot of people have questions from the waiter. They want to know whether the food is fresh, what's best on the menu, etc. How do you propose to address that?'

'It is a matter of habit, Venkat,' joined Kesam. 'When five-star hotels and high-class restaurants come up with unconventional technology, do we refuse it saying it's different? No, we do not. We are rather happy to receive better and new options. I think small restaurant owners will save money and pilferage from this venture.'

'Oh! Come on,' said Raju. 'You won't be able to convince small restaurant owners. Waiters do multi-tasking. They shop, clean and do just about everything for their hotel. The owners will never accept the technology. The bigger restaurant may accept it, but they already have similar technologies.'

But Saurabh was confident of his model. 'If we keep the device cheap, it will really help small-time restaurant owners. They can eliminate unwanted staff and keep a check on pilferage.'

Raju thought about his own restaurant and said, 'Many drunkards come to our bar at the restaurant. They spend a lot on their drinks. I would like to make a monthly or annual package for them—something like a membership card, which can be renewed from time to time.'

'Have you taken to drinking, Raju?' said Venkat mischievously. 'You must stop it now. Else you will see difficult days soon,' he guffawed as his friends started to laugh.

Kesam's plan sent all the boys laughing out so loud that they were rolling on the floor. 'I have a model of a vehicle which can run without oil. Just think of a vehicle that has legs instead of wheels.'

When she saw the boys holding their stomachs and falling off the chairs, she protested, 'You guys listen to me first. Have you seen horse's legs? Their thighs are huge, but the calves are very thin. If we make a hydraulic system wherein with every step, the upper part of the leg gets pressure due to the lower part getting pressed, a spring or dynamo could create energy enough for a small jump. When it jumps once, it will essentially come back due to gravity and, again, once it falls on its feet, it will create energy to jump again. Doing this, the machine can move long distances without wasting much energy'.

The boys calmed down and began to listen to her.

'That would be like riding a horse in a very strange way. And, how will it be controlled?' asked someone.

'I think good shock absorbers and better technology can control the machine,' she said.

Seeing everyone somewhat serious, Rohit said, 'I have 50 acres of land in north Bengal. At present, it is a tea garden. But labour cost is so high that it is difficult to maintain the tea garden. Many tea manufacturing companies have started buying tea from auctions instead of producing tea. Farming is left to the locals, so the margin has also fallen. I plan to build a palatial resort there...something like the palaces in Rajasthan. It would look like a set of a movie with beautiful interiors. People working there will dress in intricate clothes, the way they used to during the olden times,' he added.

'And you want to be the king yourself?' someone said and giggles could be heard all over the place.

'No, no. There are people who are filthy rich. I will have packages for them such as 'King for a day', 'Weekend king', or 'Good king, bad king'. 'It can be fun for visitors. Moreover, the place can be rented out for film shooting and marriages as well'.

'That's a grand idea,' said Raju, 'but have you assessed the project cost?'

'Yes, it would be around 14 to 15 crore rupees only.'

'Only?' Everybody's jaw fell as they said this in unison. Everyone knew Kesam was having an affair with Rohit, but no one knew who he was.

Amidst similar discussions, the dinner got over. The next morning they were to return to Chandigarh.

When two ends part, it is faster,

When they meet, hope delays.

Dreams are dreams, truth is truth,

Who cares what life says?

It is sad, and even at times,

It is cool then remains hot.

When we want we initiate,

Then again the wish to abort!

Meeting, mating and platonic...

Aspirations from millions again,

Sweet, sour, spicy and dull,

Feelings in deliriousness, then sane!

Why is it so complicated?

Every day welcomes new challenges...

The day started late. All the friends sat at the lobby

and had *lassi* after breakfast. 'These days there are so many hoardings on the road. The number of vehicles has also increased,' said Saurabh. 'When we came last time it was not like this. The highway is losing its charm.'

'Yes,' said Venkat. 'Also, most of the advertisements were in English earlier. Now, they are all in Hindi. It's so difficult to understand. May be, after a few years they will be in the local language. Tourists will have a hell of a problem then.'

'I would so prefer English to be our national language,' said Saurabh. This was not a comfortable topic of discussion for anyone. While one said that Tamil literature was the best, another voted for Bangla. Everyone was happy when the topic of conversation shifted to politics, population and then poetry.

When the bikes started, they took the usual detour to a temple and then visited some more quiet places. As Parwanoo got closer, Saurabh said he wanted to use a washroom.

The boys stopped near a dilapidated hotel and, leaving the bikes and Kesam on the roadside, went inside. On one side of the road were the beautiful hills and on the other a steep slope. Kesam sat on the bike and started listening to songs on her mobile phone using earphones. There was no one around. Venkat was the first to come out of the hotel. What he saw left him dumbstruck. A speeding car raced towards the bike on which Kesam was sitting and hit it hard. The car hit the bike so hard that it threw both down the hill. Venkat heard the bike crash 15 feet down. However, he did not hear the second thud.

All that Venkat could shout was the names of his friends. All rushed down the hill and saw Kesam writhing in pain and covered in blood. 'Which car was it, Venkat? What was its number?' asked Saurabh.

'The number was not written in English. It was in Hindi or something else. I could not read it.'

Five

THE ATWALS AND THE CHATWALS—Simi's dearest friend, Jassi, will get married tomorrow. After hectic shopping for the wedding, Simi sat on her bed and pulled out the laptop that hid underneath the stiff, brown shopping packets she had carelessly thrown. She immediately booked a train ticket to Ludhiana.

Varied thoughts engulfed her as soon as the laptop shut down. Jaspreet Chatwal was marrying her college friend Hardev Atwal, or Harry. The couple had seen difficult times in their relationship. Simi had been witness to everything, till she left Ludhiana for higher studies in Delhi two years ago. When the two declared to their families that they were marrying, a multitude of issues suddenly cropped up. Some may have been implacable, but many were trivial. A decision on the wedding date finally put an end to the tiresome arguments that had stretched for days between the Atwals and the Chatwals. Mutual agreements between the two families also ended the long separation between the two souls who were so much in love with each other.

Simi's thoughts started rambling to college days in Ludhiana. She vividly remembered Harry and Jassi walking hand-in-hand down the University bylanes. They made a handsome couple. Along with their thoughts, flashed the face that had never really left her memory. She felt her heart beat faster.

Kuldeep was a common friend of Simi, Jassi and Harry. Simi is still unsure if she ever had a soft corner for him. They always met as common friends. Yet, Simi's lonely heart pained when she remembered that he had left Ludhiana for Canada to do a course in hospitality management. But then, she too, had left Ludhiana for Delhi.

Simi was never able to admire Delhi. The burden of studies, long-distance travel, and the constant rush to complete trivial things, had pulled out a lot from her. She considered Delhi to be a place only for those who were born and brought up there. It was not for outsiders, she believed. It scared her to even think of living in the big, unfriendly city for a job. She saw herself a few years in the future, toiling hard from morning to night to bring home a few thousand rupees. Returning home to dark, empty rooms sent a shiver down her spine; shaking her enough to bring her back to the present.

The train left Delhi on time—six forty-five pm in the evening. As Simi settled on her seat she saw a man quite similar to Kuldeep's build sitting in the next compartment. It pained her to think of Kuldeep again and again. Why should she, she wondered? After all, they were barely friends. Rather, they had mostly avoided each other at college.

She tried to brush aside thoughts of Kuldeep. Simi had always been an average student. But she decided to pursue academics so that she could get a job and lead a life of her own choice; a life in which expenses were not something to be dealt with on a daily basis.

While shopping for the wedding, Simi had already spent more than what her pocket permitted. She started thinking about the dress she had bought for herself. But she was hardly convinced about it. It was not even yellow, her favorite colour. Years ago, Kuldeep complimented her when she wore a yellow outfit.

Again, Simi brushed away thoughts of Kuldeep.

She looked around. She felt she was shorter than most girls sitting around her. Perhaps she was heavier, too. She ran to the washroom, and stared at her face in the mirror. A sense of gloom and despondency descended on her.

Breathing the early morning air of the city she loved, freshened Simi. She was anxious to meet the bride-to-be, and as a response to her thought, called up Jassi. They chatted about the wedding trousseau. The marriage was scheduled at 11.30 am at the gurudwara. Unlike in other parts of India, marriages in Punjab usually start at around 10 am and end by 4 pm in the evening.

Simi brought out the dress she had bought for the wedding, and took not more than ten minutes to get ready. She did not look stunning, but was not unhappy with herself.

Jassi had a big and fashionably designed farmhouse. From a distance, Simi could see that the farmhouse was overly decorated. As she entered the premises, a huge gate created from bamboo sticks and pink satin drapes welcomed her. Flowers, festoons and perfumes overflowed. She saw ladies wearing costly garments and ornaments bustling in and out of the farmhouse in big modern cars.

The large hall inside the house was bustling with activity. Between shrill Bollywood songs, one could hear men shouting at those managing the decorations. Young boys, happily running from one corner to another, came in the way of caterers who were laying the line of tables for food in silver bowls.

The food, too, was exotic. Just to name a few, there was barbequed and roasted chicken with six different sauces. There was juice, chicken clear soup, Manchow soup. There were vegetable, chicken and mutton curries, salads, fruit, fresh vegetables, cream and cheese. And, of course, *gulab jamuns*, ice cream and *jalebis*.

Simi knew this place since her childhood. She also knew that both the Atwals and the Chatwals had huge debts from banks and financiers. Yet, the arrangement was majestic. She went straight to Jassi's room. It was empty, but for the packets of new dresses, gifts, bouquets and sweets strewn all across. Tea cups were littered everywhere. Someone had spilled a bottle of water on the couch. The air-conditioner was running full blast and the door was left ajar. Simi saw Jassi in the next room.

She was dressing for the parlour, which belonged to her parents. Jassi jumped on seeing Simi. It was their first meeting in three months. They hugged, kissed and shrieked. Both admired each other for having lost those extra kilos. As someone screamed at Jassi for not being ready yet, the two decided to continue the conversation on the way to the parlour.

They discussed the ornaments, the commotion outside, and how the two families agreed to the marriage. Harry had started his own business. He was prospering and had bought his own house and a factory. The otherwise laconic Simi was talking about things which she, at other times, found unimportant. But the discussions seemed too perfunctory to Simi. They touched upon one and rushed on to another.

'Who else is invited?' Simi asked suddenly on their way back home.

'If you are talking about Kuldeep, yes, he is coming,' said Jassi.

'No yaar, just wanted to know the invitees so that I get ready to meet all the elders once you have gone to the gurdwara to get married. And why did you talk about Kuldeep? I have made many friends in Delhi'.

'Oh! So now you have a Delhi guy? Tell me about him, 'Jassi carried on the conversation.

'Not one guy, I have many. They are all friends, Jassi. A couple of them are very good. But I don't see any good reason to hang around with them. I have no time,' she sighed. 'Career-wise, these are very important days for me.'

'But Kuldeep is good,' said Jassi. 'At times, I have found him more caring than Harry.'

'I have seen how boys behave in company. The moment they are alone, they become altogether different persons. Behaviour, as a pattern, changes with company.

'So you don't like Kuldeep, but he is still coming,' smiled Jassi as they reached the farmhouse. Suddenly, Simi saw a change in Jassi's persona. It was as if she had suddenly turned into a bride. Very slowly she descended from the car. A swarm of young and old ladies surrounded her, as if to protect her from all odds.

At 12.30 pm, the bride and the groom were still inside the gurdwara. Outside, the party had begun. Bagpipers, drums and the local *dhol*, all played together. The garden had caterers running around from one end to another with trays full of grilled chicken and *malai tikka*. The bar at the corner was covered with fresh flowers. When Simi spotted Kuldeep, he was already with his friends and must have downed a few pegs. She overheard him saying that the very next day he would fly back to Canada. So she would meet him just this once, she thought. Kuldeep was a short man with huge shoulders. He looked older than his age, she thought. His beard was not done completely and he did not look too great in his new blue suit. Instead of the turban, he had tied a large white handkerchief on his head.

Her limbs trembled as she began to approach him. But just then, someone called out her name. Jassi had returned from the gurdwara and had asked for Simi. The newly-wed sat in a small room closest to the garden. She congratulated the couple. Harry was dressed in an expensive suit but looked much older. "What has gone wrong with these two men?" she wondered.

By this time, the two hundred-odd people had started dancing in different groups to the cacophonous music. Most were already drunk. Their chats had become loud and animated.

'Did you talk to Kuldeep?' whispered Jassi in Simi's ears. Simi just looked into Jassi's face, after a moment's pause, she opened her confused mind to her dear friend, who had got busy smiling at the guests and could only half listen.

'You see, if you like someone, you may want to have a relationship with him. But then, at times, distance becomes a huge hurdle. You keep thinking about him when you are alone. You expect things to happen. And then you wish you had pursued it earlier.'

'Hmmm,' said Jassi. 'Did you try facebook? You should have asked me for his number.'

'No you don't understand. It's not about connecting with him again, or trying to establish a relationship. Everything has a sequence. See, if X comes before V, or A, or C in alphabets, how would it look? You first have to know someone and then have a relationship with him. You want to know how a person would behave in some situations'. 'Coincidences are missing my life, which probably creates relationships, you tell me everything in this world is so defined, what would happen if there are no coincidences, no surprises?

'But that would happen only if you make a move. Stop guessing and start talking,' was Jassi's abrupt reply.

At this moment, both heard the noise of people shouting near the bar. The commotion had compelled the musicians to lower their own music. Two well-built men were shouting at each other. Another two were holding a person who was bleeding profusely from the head. His *sherwani* had turned red with blood and his turban lay down. Two more turbans were lying near the place of action. Simi realised that a fight had picked up because of a turban that had fallen on the ground. People joined the fight. Arguments became louder. Simi realised that she had last seen the injured man with Kuldeep. And then Kuldeep appeared. He pushed a big fat man and shouted choicest expletives at him. 'Go out, go out,' he roared.

He then started attending to the injured man, who was drunk, too. For a moment Kuldeep raised his head and looked straight at Simi. But, perhaps, he did not even know who he was looking at. He returned the gaze to his injured friend and with, a few more bulky people, lifted him to the car parked outside. The injured man kept saying in a drunken, painful brawl, 'we will never be friends again, Balwant. We will never be friends again.'

Amidst broken glasses, empty plates, toothpicks and chicken bones, low music started to play again.

You passed by, I hardly saw...
Still this soft sun melted my shiver,
What melted within me I know not,
Yet I am a firm believer...

My life! for a while and me,
It resurrected whatever it could.
Your breath, this essence, was everywhere
But things happen, how they should...

Now my despair was to be near!
Now my failure wrangled me...
Once those eyes were frozen in mine
My bustling thoughts together agree

You still went by, I kept luring...
You did touch me in my thoughts

Six

THE BEGGAR—Vijayan used to work for a multinational firm in Bengaluru. But he gave up the plush job and decided to work on a government assignment that suited his passion. The new job required him to research on the boats and vessels of India. All the ancient models, all the new ones, at tiny villages, or in big cities, Vijayan must know everything about boats. So he started to travel across the country to places that have lakes, rivers, streams or seas.

This time, Vijayan had been away from home for over a year. He had seen West Bengal, Odisha, the entire coastal south, Maharashtra and Gujarat. It was early September of 1999. Settling on the seat in the train to Bengaluru, he pleasantly felt a slight nip in the air. He checked his olive green rucksack, pulled out a diary and started to flip through its pages. The diary had notes of all that Vijayan had seen on his journey. He had drawn sketches of the multifarious boats he had seen, written their measurements and shape. The shape of each boat reminded him of a specific place on the country's map. He had scribbled the name of a place next to each boat.

Vijayan was overwhelmed with the diversity of boats in India. This diversity, he thought, was because of the multiplicity of the country's geographical features and, therefore, habitats. Despite this, the number of boats had drastically reduced in the country. In most industries, giant firms have taken over small players. Boats—the oldest mode of communication—could not escape this either. New companies replaced wood with steel. Modernisation and mechanisation minimised the need for boats. In a way, this consumed the livelihood of small-time boatmen.

As Vijayan looked up, he saw a bustle of activity in the bogie. The clutter disturbed him. He went back to his diary. It gave him immense satisfaction to think that boats would be a part of his life for at least another three years—till he completed his project and submitted it to the government for the final review.

Vijayan had a special connect with boats since childhood. He remembered his tiny village in coastal Andhra Pradesh where he would run up to the sea with friends and fight to take the best place in the family boat. They would lie on it for hours and discuss the changing patterns of the clouds above. He remembered the mindless chatter he would have with friends. Friends included Mala, now his wife.

When they grew up, Vijayan and Mala decided that they wanted to spend their entire lives with each other. His friends invariably teased him about Mala. The word Vijayan means winner. 'What else will you win, now that you have won the best—Mala?' they would giggle and run away. Vijayan married Mala when he turned 30. But his friends never got tired of teasing him. Many colleagues at his earlier office were his childhood friends. 'Is child marriage still in practice?' they would laugh. Vijayan would laugh with them. Marrying to a childhood friend was child marriage for then.

He was so proud of Mala. Her beauty stunned him each time he saw her. When Vijayan was offered a job with the multinational firm, he was asked to join office at Bengaluru the next day. So Mala and their daughter, Shreya, were forced to stay back. They joined him later. 'When you go to Bengaluru, don't look at other women', Mala had told Vijayan. 'I have heard there are many north Indian girls there. They come from filthy rich families. All that they do is party and have affairs with men.' Her face had contorted when she said this. Vijayan smiled as he remembered her expression, and almost laughed when he recollected Mala saying that all north Indian women were fair and that all men think that 'fair is better'.

His heart was full of love and gratitude for Mala. Life must be so boring for Mala when he was away for months. But then, she could not go anywhere. Vijayan's family owned a temple, which must be looked after. He remembered what Mala had said when he was leaving for

Bengaluru. 'Every woman is like a boat. She must be tied to something so that she feels safe. She needs an anchor so that she can acquire the freedom that she otherwise cannot get.'

The train reached its destination on time. As everyone rushed to alight from the train first, Vijayan collected his bags. The bags mostly comprised gifts he had bought for Mala and Shreya. He felt them by touching the bags rom outside and smiled. He was anxious to reach home.

As the rickshaw pulled up outside his house, he saw fresh paint on the walls outside. A new TV antenna stood tall at the rooftop. So now he would be able to get all the news, he thought. As he entered home, Shreya ran up to him and climbed straight into his sturdy arms. Mala, too, did a short sprint and clung to him. Both Mala and Shreya were like two fruits on a plant. The family was together again. They discussed the cold, hard idli and flat chutney that Vijayan was forced to eat on the train. How relieved Vijayan was to think that he would get delicious food cooked by Mala.

Mala had always told Vijayan that she loved to be with him. One reason for this was his physical strength, she said. Vijayan had saved Mala at various instances—once from a bad tempered cow. Each time she spoke about this, she would start talking about the man who made the couple get married. Was there a connection? Vijayan always wondered, but never asked.

She called him uncle, but he was not related to her. All the children in the village called him uncle. He had come from Chennai and worked at a homeopathic clinic. But one fine day he left the place without informing anyone. That was 22 years ago. She told Vijayan that she wanted to meet him at least once to thank him for helping them get married.

As night started covering everything in darkness, people and animals shrank into their cosy corners. After dinner, Vijayan emptied his rucksack and started placing his books and papers on the study table. He also carefully kept the diary he had been reading in the train. Mala and Shreya peered eagerly at the diary. Shreya was not interested in boats, but was keen on seeing the diary. This diary was almost a travelogue. It had stories of people far and wide. People Vijayan found distinct were all inside this diary. He would draw their pencil sketches and write a small note on how they were unique. Vijayan's art work was vivid and lively.

He laughed at Shreya's curiosity and picked up the diary. As he reached the bed, the two ladies followed him. She hurried to open the diary, and almost instantly a string of giggles followed. There was the sketch of a man from Tamil Nadu who used to sleep in his boat. That was his job! Shreya pointed at the man's large ears and laughed out aloud. Then there was the man from West Bengal. His very long nose looked funny. There were many faces Vijayan had drawn this time. His stories about them stretched for long. Each time Mala turned the diary towards her to look at the sketches, Shreya would pull it back.

Vijayan began the story about the priest from Punjab

who was ill-treated by his son. Shreya seemed engrossed in the story, so Mala pulled the diary to herself. When she turned the page, the sketch that stared at her left her numb. Vijayan had drawn the face she remembered so vividly. Next to the sketch the scribble was hardly legible. She strained her eyes to read it, but could not. 'You want to hear about him first?' asked Vijayan.

'No,' she said. 'I have already heard so many stories by now. Just tell me his name. Then I will go inside the kitchen for a few minutes and prepare Shreya's school tiffin for tomorrow.'

'He is Praveen Kumar, a mad beggar. I found him begging at a zoo in Odisha. I figured he was from the South and enquired about him. Someone told me he had once locked himself up in a cage in a circus. Doctors have declared him mentally ill. He keeps muttering strange things.'

Do you care to look at me?

My filthy corner has a lot...

I don't need a family now,

In deep sleep, I dream what not?

Your endless toil takes you nowhere

Money and machines are a waste,

However friends you may have made,

Without hunger, where is taste?

Look, family gives you pain.

Whatever you do, they'll call it vain…

Is there a point in living like this?

In hugs and tears, you roll again…

I the beggar, of the street ask,

How fortunate are you, my dear?

Mala stood up and with wobbly feet headed straight for the kitchen. Shreya had fallen asleep by now. Vijayan carefully placed her on a soft pillow and covered her with a thin linen sheet. He then tip-toed to the kitchen and hugged his wife from behind. To his surprise, he felt Mala sobbing. Caught unawares, Mala controlled herself and started talking about how her eating habits had changed.

Vijayan was worried seeing her tears and asked her innumerable times the cause of her distress. But he got no credible reply. 'Is Praveen Kumar the uncle you had been looking for?' he asked curiously.

'Of course not,' was Mala's terse reply.

Many a time, Women are often happy and sad without a reason, thought Vijayan. The fatigue of the journey made him reach up to the bed. He was asleep instantly.

The sketch had agonised Mala immensely. Of course, she knew Praveen Kumar. She also knew that he was the one whom children so lovingly called Uncle. She always wanted to meet him. But that was not out of gratitude. It was to take revenge. The night had suddenly become darker for Mala. She pulled herself to the bed and cried inconsolably as she remembered how the beast had molested her at his homeopathic clinic when she was all of 13.

Seven

THE CRADLE AND THE GRAVE—It had poured for three consecutive days. The day broke with the noisy croak of toads. Trees drooped from the weight of rainwater. Pavements were full of snails whose shells had been smashed by pedestrians. It rained relentlessly and the sky seemed to be apologising for the sudden demise of these tiny creatures. Soil along on the pavements had become home to seedlings that had begun to sprout. Each seedling had given way to two tiny leaves. They looked as if they were folding hands, asking for forgiveness from man for having doubted their love for plants.

Morning had started its everyday murmur. Couples had started to sip their bed tea and bachelors yearned for company to enjoy the beauty of nature. Social vigils were also up and loudly exchanged pleasantries from each other's balconies. 'It's raining heavily, isn't it?' While one said it was the 'monsoon rains' another made superfluous comments. 'It started on a Saturday you see, so it will not stop till next Saturday.' In eastern India, many believe that when it starts to rain on a Saturday, it stops only after a week.

In this clean, hot and humid city of Bhubaneswar, rains had come very early this year; so early that no one was sure if it was the monsoon. But surely, it mesmerised each one.

Little Swati sat on a chair in the balcony watching the bounties of nature. She could feel minute droplets fall on her face. Cool, light breeze played with her hair and repeatedly fell on her cheeks even as she placed them back behind her ears. The wind played with her as a passionate lover. There were men and women walking down the street, some in raincoats and others under the umbrella. She craned her neck to peep into her neighbour's room. As she had expected, her dear friend Payal was lying prostate on the bed sound asleep. Swati wished it would stop raining now.

Swati and Payal, both, would not go to school because of the rains. All that Swati wanted to do now was reach Payal's room and shake her out of bed. Every holiday Payal would sleep till late. That's because she would be up till late at night.

Swati's mother now called her to the dining table for breakfast, and scolded her for wetting her face. 'This is just a sprinkle of water,' Swati protested.

'Well, the one who does not love the rains is a murderer at heart,' said Swati's father at the breakfast table.

'Oh! Really? Does that mean all those who want to dry their clothes under the sun are murderers?' laughed her mother. And the two broke into laughter that was triggered more by the pleasant weather than the conversation.

The conversations that followed mainly revolved around the weather and carried the similar happy tone. Imbued by the happiness, Swati, too, felt a tinge of happiness. She quickly finished her breakfast and went to the balcony once again. This time she felt something beautiful about the rains. She admired the spherical droplets that fell over the flowerpots.

'Rains are a boon for every living creature on this earth,' she thought. Her mind wandered. 'What would life be without water?' She thought of a sailor lost in the ocean without a drop of water to drink. Her throat parched. She then thought of the desert. 'What a torture it must be to live in a desert! And what if one got lost in it?' She shivered at the thought. She stretched out her little hands and was comforted by the heavy drops of water that fell on them.

Swati developed an urge to write. The first thing that came to her mind was poetry. But she remembered when her English teacher had asked each student in class to write a poem on their mothers. She remembered how she had gone nuts trying to rhyme every sentence. So should it be an essay? 'It would be so boring to write an essay at home. It would be like doing homework,' she said to herself. It is too tedious to write an essay, she frowned.

So a painting it must be. Swati remembered the art exhibition her father had recently taken her to. The painting of a spaniel who had taken shelter under a broken chair placed beside a closed door had etched in her mind. Swati snapped her fingers in delight, rushed inside her room and brought out a drawing paper, colours and paint brush. 'I will draw a calf taking shelter under our car garage. What a magnificent idea!'

Within about half an hour, she had completed her painting. She took a step back to admire it. 'No, the calf does not resemble a pig,' she said to herself, and picked it up to show it to her elder brother, Atul. Every time she drew something, she would show it to him for approval. Atul was engrossed in a crime thriller. He glanced at the painting, murmured 'hmm', and went back into the book. Swati had to shake him so that he could see her accomplishment. This time Atul looked at it, smiled and then asked, 'What is it?' Swati blushed and said, 'It's a calf in our garage'. Atul laughed aloud and said, 'So why don't you give a caption under the painting, 'Calf caught in the rain'?' The little girl did not catch her brother's sarcasm and immediately wrote it down.

'Swati,' her mother called out seeing paint spilled all over the floor in her room.

'This is what you do when you don't go to school,' she scolded. 'Open your books at once. I will come in 15 minutes and ask you what Rip Van Winkle saw when he woke up after 20 years of slumber'.

Swati wanted to show her work of art to her father who loved her so. But he was already off to work. It was a long day for Swati as she waited for him to return. When he came, two of his friends trooped in, too. She held back her anxiety for some time. When she could hold no more, she plunged into the sofa and opened her masterpiece in front of her father's face. Her father shoved her aside gently and told her that he would see it later.

Swati's mother laid the table with tea and biscuits, and discussions began. It seemed to be a continuation of debate left mid-way. One of the two friends said, 'You know, aesthetics plays a vital role in our lives. People like or dislike characters from their own aesthetics. See, when new neighbours shift to our locality, people whose characters are similar to theirs try to connect with them. This is because of aesthetics. Then again, if you talk about a person—good or bad—you relate that person to character you already know,' he sipped tea and continued.

'In different societies, countries or geographical locations, an important contribution comes from aesthetics alone in terms of understanding of characters. We read books, watch movies, reality shows and plays. The characters that we see or read emerge from the author's own aesthetics. We learn from them how characters can be different. They look different, think different, and have different relationships. Their responses in families and among friends are also different.'

'I totally agree,' said Swati's father. 'Another contribution to aesthetics is art. Art is a reflection of society. There are not many who get the privilege to understand aesthetics through art. What I feel sad about is that in India women have made very few contributions to art, barring in the last three or four decades. It makes understanding them difficult. There should be some contribution from women of all societies to aesthetics. Societies that do not have their contribution face problems in terms of understanding. And then women complain that men don't understand women,' they all laughed together. Swati's mother, who had just left the kitchen to go to Atul's room, stopped to respond. But could not, as the other friend had already started to talk. She walked away.

'You see, it is not unusual that one set of people's thoughts differ from another set's. But at such times, one set must follow the norms that are accepted by society at large. So in many countries we see cruelty, suppression and hardships. It could be because of religion, sex, money or anything else. Those who follow the norms are shown as examples of 'good girls', 'good ladies', 'good fathers', etc. These 'good' people do what they may or may not like. But they definitely do not do what they like. This is where our country lags'.

'Today some parents think that they are smart enough

to put the girl kid in any educational which promises for a "safe" job, this is blasphemy of the education system, it keeps your fifty percent of the population in dreams.'

Sitting on the sofa, Swati listened to the discussion wide-eyed. She had understood absolutely nothing, but knew that the discussion would take very long to end. She went inside her room with her masterpiece and sat on the reading chair.

You the face, you know I love,

You the heart, I know you can,

See where we culminate…

Envisage where we began.

Ruling the roost, this hullabaloo,

Expectations and harsh breach,

Lost love and forgotten faith,

This kid, and you cannot reach.

I am living I shall breathe.

So shall you on your notion,

Finding oneself knowing something,

Moving ahead in this commotion…

This shapely acceptance, and trust,

May remain forever between us...

It was almost night now. Swati went to the balcony again. She could see ants that had left their flooded holes and were now flying whereever there was light. She could see that frogs were delighted at the sight of so many insects around. Her feet felt the water that the rain had left on the balcony. But she was not thinking of the rains any longer. As she waited for her father's friends to leave, she stretched out her hands under the open sky. This time, it remained dry.

Eight

STORY OF MEN—It was raining that December evening in Shimla. Chilly winds from the snow-capped Himalayas had numbed each toe in the city. The approaching dark night had done its best to increase the dullness which poverty had brought about in the life of Sudhir. Food seemed the only solace.

He dropped a few biscuits on a plate and made tea for himself. Absence of company was too painful on this dark, morose evening. The relationship between food and company, he thought, was symbiotic. He desperately needed someone to talk to, someone who could hear him talk; may be just about how the day went. How unfortunate he was to be away from home. It was almost seven months now. Sudhir looked at the biscuits and tea. His empty stomach growled. Within minutes he had devoured them all.

Sudhir's parents lived in a small village in the Kinnaur district of Himachal Pradesh. He had travelled 250 kilometres to Shimla in the early summer of 2012 to join his first job in a telecommunication company. Since then, homesickness stuck to him like a disease. The road that led to his home beckoned him umpteen times. Oh! That cosy bed, the tempting smell of mother's food, and the chatter of friends. He missed them all so much. But his resolve stopped him from running home.

Sudhir had promised himself to go home only after losing the probation tag from his designation. He wanted to be a permanent employee in the company. Well, his supervisor had told him in the morning that his confirmation letter had been despatched from Mumbai. Would he get an increment too, he wondered! His parents would be so proud of him if he reached home with a permanent job and a salary hike, he thought while adjusting his collar.

As a child, Sudhir made all possible efforts to do well in studies and make his parents proud. But he could never rise above the average. His father retired from a private company 15 years ago. The company had no pension policy. The family had no other source of earning and lived in penury. Sudhir gave his parents immense happiness with a new source of income. He sent home most of his monthly salary. But it was not enough. Giving them the basic comforts of life was a colossal task for him. Ailing health and a crumbling house could be looked after later.

He felt dejected, and thought about some of his friends who were successful. They could turn cash to gold. But he was not one of them. He would accept life as it came. His dream did not go beyond having a stable salary and being able to pull his family out of the poverty dungeon.

Night had descended. It was still pouring. Through the window Sudhir could see the frame of a short man holding an umbrella and a small white bag approaching his house. It was Chaudhary. Sudhir never understood why Chaudhary came to his place so often. While he was still in his twenties, Chaudhary was a middle-aged man. He was born and brought up in a small village in Chamba, H.P. where his mother lived. His father was in the Indian Army and would get posted at different locations across the country every three years. Chaudhary had spent some part of his life in Chandigarh with his father.

He worked at the Public Works Department. The two got to know each other about seven months ago when Sudhir was looking for a house in Shimla. Chaudhary had convinced the landlord to ask for a small rent. He helped Sudhir settle in the new place and started dropping in at least once a week with a bottle of rum in one hand and a packet of fried nuts in the other. His wife hated his drinking habit. As Sudhir lived alone, the best place to meet was this small house. There was no disagreement on this.

Sudhir disliked him. He hated his mindless chit chat. He disliked his job, too. In fact, he envied it. It paid him so well. Sudhir saw Chaudhary enter home, once again with alcohol and snacks. He was trying to find a place to keep the umbrella. His long, fair face shone through the darkness. His nose was unusually short and bent towards his right. For Sudhir, this man was a waste of time. Once drunk, he would dislike everything under the sun. And he would be very vocal about it. Sudhir could easily tell him to leave. But the sight of rum made him smile. And then again, company is better than solitude. Perhaps, this is how relationships are up in the hills. Life is hard for everyone in difficult terrain. With very few options, people settle for whatever they get.

The two smiled at each other and sat down to spend the evening together. Discussions began about the rains and the bone-chilling winter winds. Naldehra, just a few kilometres from Shimla, had witnessed snowfall in the morning. Before the discussion was over, Chaudhary had started talking about water scarcity...and then about public rage that injured some priests. Chaudhary would change the topic of discussion by every minute.

He had now started talking about a book he had recently finished reading. 'The protagonist did not believe in God. He was a strong man,' Chaudhary said. 'He made his life a success because of his own worth. He helped everyone who needed his help. He loved his wife and children. But he never prayed.'

'I really liked his character. So I keep narrating extracts from this book to my friends. The writer is a real philosopher. The way he has written it, all the incidents seem extremely real, so real that one can start living it. Listen to this short poem from the book:

Faith is omnipresent
In all shapes, colours and abstract
Some carry it from the womb
Some acquire it by some tact

When I talk to myself I say,
There is this joy and there is dismay!
This faith in me, this ambrosia!
My belief in pangs of amnesia...

My God you are a person, are you?
Why do I go back and fall?
Now and then I keep running
Then again you stand so tall!

You can be with me as you are
As people have taught and fought.'

Chaudhary picked up his glass and drew himself towards Sudhir. His eyes dilated and his voice lowered. 'It's all meaningless. So many people die every day. Religion is the culprit in most of these deaths. I say, why can't I forget religion? Forget the very concept of God? Here, I'm not talking of Communism or Marxism. I'm simply talking of the life that we live every day—life in the same house, the same country, eating the same *roti* and *daal* and talking to the same set of people, but after forgetting religion.'

The volume of Chaudhary's voice had started to increase. Rum had started pumping his blood faster. He took another sip from his glass and with knitted brows, looked straight into his eyes. Sudhir knew Chaudhary was about to ask him something related to religion.

'Tell me, what do you do every day for your religion apart from bowing for five minutes? Many of us do not even do this. There are only a few women who pray for hours in the absence of anything better to do. But do they fight in communal clashes?'

'No', said Sudhir.

'So it can be deduced that those who pray less fight more?'

'No', said Sudhir.

'So what do you call a person who does not pray, yet fights for his religion?'

'I think it is about identity and not religion. I would prefer to use the word faith instead of religion. Faith is like a new shirt which must be kept properly or else it will keep bothering you. Our holy books tell us how to lead good lives. Man is a social animal and these stories keep us together. They stop us from doing any harm to society as a whole,' said Sudhir.

'Holy books? Which holy book are you talking about? These are story books written extremely well with the intention of sounding aesthetic. A writer always tries to convey his ideas to the reader by relating them to his surroundings. When the story is unrelated to his surroundings, it is science fiction written only to entertain. Evidence has been found of all that was written in the so-called holy books. Authors of these books referred to the ruins of old cities, towns, monuments and palaces to give people references.'

'Had I been born somewhere else or in any other religion, I would have been equally passionate or dispassionate about God, religion, home, country,' continued Chaudhary.

'So you believe that holy books are differently written fiction. And that everything is fiction once the fear of God, or life after death, is removed.'

'No, it's not like that. A person must be associated with someone in terms of faith, be it God or a person. It could even be a place or a thing which he likes. You are correct. God is, perhaps, the most common of all these. May be for the sake of humanity religion is needed'.

Chaudhary's face suddenly lit up. 'Have you seen the tigers and lions etched in stone in our temples? They barely resemble the actual tigers and lions. I am sure their artists would never have seen those big animals in real life. When the sculptures were made, there was no television or newspapers. They must have seen others' sculptures and sketches and given them facial expressions.'

'Ha ha ha...this is funny,' laughed Sudhir. The ring of Chaudhary's mobile phone broke the conversation. Sudhir knew it was his wife. He gulped down the last sip in his glass and picked himself up. He carefully tied the umbrella which had dried by now and said goodbye, leaving the door open to allow the wind to come in and let the rum out of Sudhir's senses.

It was late. He needed to cook dinner. When he got up, he saw a piece of paper lying on the floor. It was the same chit from which Chaudhary had read out the poem.

He knew that Chaudhary's son has died recently in an accident, while he pities him, he still envied him.

Nine

BARIATRIC SURGERY—Rahul Sharma was a friend to almost everyone he knew. An extremely talkative person and very good at heart, he had a big circle of friends in Delhi—the place where he was born and brought up. Everyone knew him to be a self-made man.

He had had his share of struggle as a child, but overcame them on his own. His father had a small business in auto parts. When Rahul was barely 15 years old, his father survived a paralytic attack. Doctors said he had suffered cerebral thrombosis. He could no longer work. Rahul's two sisters, who were pursuing higher education, left studies and took up small-time jobs so that the family could get a regular income. Rahul was still in school, so he was not allowed to work.

As time went by, his sisters started teaching in school and earned money from tuitions as well. They were able to get married without monetary help from the family. But after the sisters left home, running the house was impossible. They did send clothes and money but it was not enough. Rahul's fees would regularly get delayed. Eventually, his mother sold her ornaments; then they shifted to a small, rented accommodation and rented their own big house. They used the money to run the house. For education, Rahul took a student's loan.

Time also saw his father's condition improve. The doctor would come home each day, tie a rope to two trees and make him walk holding the help of the rope. Soon, he was walking holding a stick. One day, his father's friend told him that he should throw the stick away. 'Your children are not old enough to take care of you right now,' he said. The sentence pained Rahul no end, but it made his father walk on his own.

When Rahul graduated, in 1999, his father had started walking properly. He started another shop. By this time, Rahul's circle of friends had widened immensely. His friends would listen to his jokes, give him an ear when he was sad, and support him whenever he needed it. But with too many friends came too many bad habits as well. Alcohol and parties became a part of his life.

In 2002, Rahul got a job at a call centre in Gurgaon. His calibre helped him shift to the KPO industry soon. He secured a senior position in a Gujarat-based unlisted company. The company had full faith in his capabilities and one day gave him quite a few of the company's shares. If the company got listed, it would change his and his family's life.

That day when Rahul returned home, he told his father to stop working. The words of his father's friend, 'Your children are not old enough to take care of you,' still reverberated in his mind. He was now happy that he could take care of his family. He sold the shop to his uncle for a meagre amount as he, too, was going through bad times.

Meanwhile, Rahul fell in love and got married. He had seen his sisters not take a paisa from their father when they married. He wanted to do the same. So he took a loan from a bank. Repayment was not a problem. After all, he would be a big man once his company got listed, he thought. Then, he would repay the loans taken for his father's shop, his own education, for marriage and for the house he had bought after marriage.

Rahul felt satisfied. He knew he had established himself in the industry. At home there was happiness, too. He had been able to bring back his parents to their own big house and live there with his wife and two children. To achieve all this, he had many debts, but then he had ample confidence, too, that his company would get listed and he would be able to repay all loans.

At parties, between drinks, he would speak to his friends about the shares. They all knew he was successful. On one such evening, he got a phone call from an old school friend. 'Hey Fatty, how are you? How many kilos have you added to your belly?' he asked cheerfully.

People had called Tushar Sehgal 'fatty' since he was a child. Just about a year ago when Rahul had met him in

Jaipur, he had crossed 160 kg. 'I am suffering from OSA,' said Tushar over the phone. 'It means Obstructive Sleep Apnea. Doctors have suggested bariatric surgery,' the words pierced through Rahul's drunken brain like a sharp arrow. 'My obesity is a big problem now. I am not able to sleep. I used a machine to sleep for six months. Now even the machine is not much help. I fall asleep while driving. My family is extremely worried about me,' he said.

'OK, let me call you back,' he said and immediately drove home. The word 'surgery' kept ringing in his ears.

On reaching home, he went straight to the shower and tried to clear his head. He called Tushar back.

'But you are insured, right? Get operated as soon as possible,' he said. Tushar explained the predicament to him.

'It's a lifestyle issue, brother. Insurance companies do not pay for bariatric surgery. One of my relatives has given me Rs 50,000. The surgery has been scheduled for next week. I have no idea from where I will get the total sum of Rs 5 lakh.'

Rahul knew that Tushar was not financially well off. He had worked hard to get his sister married. His younger brother was still studying.

'Why did he eat so much and reach this condition?' Rahul thought to himself angrily. He called up his doctor friend and discussed the case. 'Surgery is the only option,' the doctor confirmed.

Rahul did not have Rs 5 lakh. In fact, he had not been

able to save anything because of loans. He was in no position to take another loan. But then, this was March. By April, his company would give him performance pay. He thought about his shares and felt strength seep into his tired body. Something came to his mind and he rushed to his laptop.

He opened a new Facebook account and named it 'Help Tushar Sehgal'. He added all his school friends in the group. By next morning around 30 people had responded enquiring about Tushar. Friends from across the country and abroad started calling Rahul. He painstakingly explained to each one about OSA and bariatric surgery. In bariatric surgery the stomach is cut to reduce appetite. Each time he would say this, his own stomach would pain. He also told them not to tell Tushar about the website, or else he might get hurt. The next day was all about taking calls and answering messages. Most were sympathetic. Those who were not in touch with Tushar laughed at his weight. By the evening, many had committed to pay. As usual, Rahul felt proud of himself.

So when Tushar called up the next morning, Rahul said, 'I am trying to arrange the money, buddy. Go ahead with the surgery'. When he went to work, he opened his computer and immediately posted his account number in the group so that the process of transferring the contribution could be simplified. Though no contribution came that day, the next day Rs 10,000 was transferred by one of Tushar's closest friends. 'Arranging money takes time, so they may take time to contribute,' he thought to himself. But Tushar's operation could not wait. Rahul decided to take it all upon himself.

He called up a friend in Dubai and asked for four lakh forty thousand rupees with the promise to repay it within a month. He would get a salary raise next month and then, shares were coming his way soon. Within an hour Rahul had the amount in his bank account. He immediately sent the money to Tushar. He felt proud and content that he had been able to help his friend in time of need. To celebrate his success he went to the bar with his office colleagues. They admired his confidence.

The day Tushar was operated, Rahul stood beside his family. When doctors declared the surgery a success, he was ecstatic. Without even meeting Tushar, he rushed out to the bar. Anyway, he had been told that Tushar would regain consciousness only the next day.

The next day, Rahul opened the 'Help Tushar Sehgal' account. No one had transferred a paisa. And the next day was just as bad. He started posting reminders along with his account number in the group. Yet, no one responded.

Rahul would have met a slim Tushar when the hospital relieved him. But someone from office phoned him that an urgent meeting had been called. So he rushed to Gurgaon. Meeting Tushar became impossible, as he was to return to Jaipur. After the surgery, some mutual friends met Tushar at the hospital. They told him that Rahul had not been alone in paying the operation amount. They told him about the Facebook account. Tushar reached Jaipur thinking that a group of friends had collected the amount to pay to the hospital. He would take time and pay them one by one, he thought.

That day in office, Rahul was told that the company made very low profits that financial year and there would neither be any annual increment nor any performance pay. In fact, some people would be removed.

What more can one give?
Beyond his own capacity?
Then there is a hollow need,
Yet people arrange charity.

There is this me against all odds,
My well-being a mere hope,
Beyond my arms I want to reach,
Sagacity with over-confidence elope.

True meaning of respite is not,
To pass on the pain from one.
Repose remains the best when,
Generosity troubles none.

This charity is beyond reasons,
Till it is beyond resources.

Rahul could see his life crashing in front of his eyes. The Facebook account saw no more contributions. He took a loan to repay his friend in Dubai. When Tushar felt slightly better in Jaipur, he called up Rahul and asked for the list of people who had contributed. 'I will pay them back in two years,' he said.

Now, Rahul does not drink or party. He knows that one can give happiness only if one has it himself.

Ten

AN OLD SIN—'It's a girl!' Vimal sent the message to all his relatives and friends through his cell phone. His ecstasy knew no bounds.

That night he blissfully wrote in his diary, 'I will name her Naina. I hope she loves me the most.' Vimal had married Shweta at the age of 31. The baby came about six years later. After the long wait, Naina came as a bundle of joy.

As he reminisced on the baby's arrival in this big bad world, he wrote, 'It was early June. Shweta woke up with an unusual pain in the abdomen. It took me some time to understand that she was in labour and needed a doctor immediately. I hastily phoned the office, asked for leave and rushed her to the hospital. Dr Vani Thapar, her gynaecologist for the past nine months, had said that Shweta should have a normal baby. Today, after I had spent about six hours waiting nervously outside the labour room, Dr Thapar came out and said the baby wasn't coming out. Shweta would have to deliver the baby through caesasean.

'I had no clue what the doctor was talking about. I looked at my friend Pallab, who was a resident doctor and had sat next to me the whole day. He explained to me that Shweta needed an operation.

'I knew nothing about caesarean, just as I knew nothing about a normal delivery. Shweta was now entirely in the doctors' hands. I gave my approval on Pallab's advice. Shweta was rushed to the operation theatre. After a good one-and-a-half hours, Dr Thapar came to me holding an angel in her hands. It was my Naina. My princess looked straight into my eyes. She filled my heart with love and compassion. At that time, I did not know that I would love this girl more than anyone else in this world.'

What we want remains a dream, my child,
What we have, we do not value.
Forever these dreams are chased,
Routine toil is never appraised.

Be content, my child, I shall die,
The end is the same for both of us.
Smaller things in life are grand,
Everything else is another errand.

Hope to remain happy with nature,

The mother, the creator of all.

See, you always have friends along,

The sound of breath is the best song.

I can save what is already there,

You save it for the rest of souls.

Vimal and Shweta belonged to average Indian families. They were affluent because of their own well-earning jobs. They had spent a lot of money to build their house, and even more to turn the house into home. It had all kinds of technology-driven equipment. The two had remained so engrossed in building their own professional careers, that they thought that the arrival of a baby would hinder their career growth. Later when they decided it was time to have a family, nature would not have it their way. So when Naina came six years after marriage, both were in a state of euphoria.

However, bringing up a child is no mean task for working couples. Soon both realised that as working parents, life was more like a war zone. The fight was between being good professionals and good parents. At work, competition was so stiff that eventually the profession would first start gnawing you and then devour you wholly, leaving nothing of you for the family.

Vimal did not quite understand how working women should lead their lives after becoming mothers. He, like his parents, believed that children should be brought up under their mothers' care. But he also believed, like his wife, that women must work.

We all argue during coffee table debates that women need to be independent and must have their own jobs. According to statistics, they comprise a major portion of the unemployed youth in India. Each father wants his girl child to be well-educated and get the best possible job. In the past three or four decades, many working women have been very successful, but many more are so caught up in their domestic lives that freedom is too far a cry. Still many families make girl child go for education which would fetch them a safer job, an 'office only' kind of job.

When Shweta's three months of maternity leave got over, she became impatient to resume work. Vimal, too, had joined work after 15 days of paternity leave. At office, Vimal's friend, Tanuj, asked matter-of-factly, 'So what will happen to Naina once your wife resumes work? You parents live far away. Who will look after her?' Tanuj was lucky. He never had to bother about bringing up his son. His wife was not working and his parents stayed with him.

'My wife earns enough to pay for the baby-sitter as well as for the domestic help,' he said, rather too proudly. But within his heart, he knew nothing as to what would happen to Naina, the love of his life. 'Leaving her to a baby-sitter?' He shivered at the thought.

That day, Vimal entered home with an electrician. He had bought a CCTV module which the electrician would install. He reassured himself that with this device, they would manage with a baby-sitter.

A day before Shweta's maternity leave was over, she got a phone call from the office. She must join work the next day, they said. Vimal reached home late that day. He had a long evening meeting with Tanuj because they had to finalise a big deal with a client on the outskirts of the city the next day.

Naina giggled at him when he picked her up in his arms. She hit her tiny hands in the air and played with Vimal's fingers for some time. Soon, she was sound asleep. He kept her carefully on the bed and went up to Shweta. 'Must you join tomorrow? We have not planned it yet,' he muttered.

'Oh! I had called up an agency and got a list of baby-sitters in the morning. I met four of them. One of them was fine. I gave the agency advance money so that she could start from tomorrow itself.'

'But who is she? How did you find her fine? I am worried,' he tried to say.

'Don't worry, she is about 50 years old and knows some cooking as well. When I met her, I left Naina with her for some time. They both seemed comfortable,' she said.

'All right, if it's settled then I will drop you to the

office tomorrow at 9.30 am. What time will the baby-sitter come?'

'She should get here by 8 am. Her name is Kamla.'

'What a common name! Were you really satisfied after meeting her? Look, I cannot take leave tomorrow to keep a watch on her. My team and I have to sign a big deal tomorrow.'

'Don't worry, dear. This had to happen someday,' Shweta tried to comfort him.

They discussed how finances would be managed till late at night. Both agreed that it was imperative for Shweta to work if they needed to move forward in their lives. It was good for them, for Naina, and for their parents, they thought. At night, however, Vimal convinced Shweta to call her mother home to keep an eye on the baby-sitter.

The next day, as Vimal was getting ready for the day, he could hear Kamla and his mother-in-law discuss the dos and don'ts of babysitting. When he came out of his room for breakfast, he saw Kamla for the first time. She was unusually fair and despite her age looked extremely beautiful and vibrant. He thought she must be from a good family and felt Naina would be safe in her hands.

But something troubled him at the back of his mind. Kamla had a black scar on the neck. He thought he had seen it before. Had he seen her before as well? The thought kept nagging him as he chewed his chapatti on the breakfast table. Her laughter seemed rather mischievous now.

The couple left home. Vimal dropped Shweta to her office. On leaving she said she would reach home late. It was her first day after three months, so it was expected of her to work till late.

To sign the big deal, Vimal and Tanuj left for the city's suburbs. They reached the meeting place in the afternoon. It took them some time to close the deal. When it was signed, both were very happy as it would give huge returns. The deal involved heavy paperwork and it took till the evening to finish.

When they started to return to their homes, Vimal realised that the batteries of his cell phone as well as the laptop were dying. He had left the chargers of both beside the bed and had forgotten to pick them up while coming to office. At this time, Shweta called to say that her work was over and he could pick her up now. She told him that her mother had left and Naina was alone with Kamla. But Vimal would take another two hours to reach. Suddenly anger overpowered Vimal's senses. He told her sharply to take a cab and rush home. When he saw Tanuj uncomfortably listening to the conversation, he lowered his voice.

After leaving home, Vimal and Shweta had constantly called home asking how Naina was. They saw her actions through the CCTV. But all this happened only till the first half of the morning. Later, both got busy with work and found no time to call home.

At 6.30 pm, Vimal realised that the phone would be dead within minutes. He called up Shweta to say that she could contact him on Tanuj's phone.

This was the time Vimal had feared ever since the couple planned a child. Deep in his heart, he was always uncomfortable leaving home a small child alone with just the baby-sitter. Newspapers and magazines were full of horrifying stories about crèches. 'Why on earth did mom-in-law leave so early? Why could I not take leave today? Why did Shweta have to join today? She could have waited for some more days, at least till Naina grew up.' The thoughts were slowly pulling him towards the world of fear and threat. His fear for Naina's safety grew bigger and bigger.

Tanuj had never seen Vimal so tense. 'Why are you so worried? Nothing will happen to her. These days baby-sitters take good care of children,' he said trying to comfort him. But Tanuj was not aware what was troubling Vimal since morning. The whole day Kamla's face flashed through his mind. Where had he seen her before? The thought was persistent and troublesome.

As Vimal and Tanuj drove on the highway, Vimal's tired and scared mind took a short nap. When he woke up, they had reached Delhi. He looked at his phone. It was dead. So he asked Tanuj for his phone. This time, Shweta's phone was switched off. 'Tanuj, let's please call the police,' he said.

'Police? Why are you so worried, man? All must be well. Let Shweta reach home, she will call back, I'm sure. Or, you can call a neighbour if you have the number,' Tanuj said.

'My phone is switched off. I don't remember any phone number,' he said helplessly.

'Come on, tell me. What do you fear?'

'I was all of 16 then,' Vimal started abruptly. 'My parents and elder brother had gone to Ludhiana to attend a marriage. In the evening some friends of my brother came to my house and said that an aunt was looking for a place to spend the night. I let her stay at my house till the morning. But I soon realised that the boys were not well-intentioned. They spent at least four hours with her in my brother's closed room. After the boys left, she called me in and tried to seduce me. She must have been 30 then. After a few years I realised that she may have been a prostitute. Tanuj, I think Kamla is the same woman.'

'In the morning when I saw her, I was not sure who she was. Now, I am sure,' Vimal continued. 'I am sure she means to harm Naina. Oh God! Why did I not realise this earlier?' he cried holding his head in both his hands.

'Tanuj, please do something. I cannot speak to my wife. I am sure something is wrong at home,' he pleaded.

Taken aback by Vimal's sudden confession, Tanuj sat still for a while. He then said, 'I don't think a woman would be bad just because she was once a prostitute. And even if she is a bad woman, she has been referred by the agency. We can call the agency to know more about her.'

'No,' said Vimal. 'Shweta had met the people in the agency. She would not like such a discussion.' Just then Tanuj's phone rang. It was Shweta. Amidst Naina's gurgles, he heard Shweta say that she was home. Kamla had left only after helping Shweta with the dinner preparation.

That night, Shweta asked Tanuj to join them for dinner. They had long discussions on parenting and baby-sitters across the city.

Eleven

LEMONS AND DEMONS—Amit, Ketan and Shiv were inseparable since high school. Not one day would pass without the three speaking to each other. Meeting was possible only now and then. So when Ketan returned disappointed from his honeymoon, they had to meet. Amit called up Ketan and asked what had happened.

'It ended too soon,' he moaned even as Amit laughed out loud.

Call it budget constraint or unavailability of leave from office, Ketan and Palak had to return to Kolkata from Malaysia within 15 days. Married for just about a month, they had loved their stay in the Southeast Asian country. But they wanted more of the fun and hated to return.

'Can't we go out again? We could go somewhere in India itself, may be Manali,' Palak had suggested while packing lunch for office.

'Yes, let's do that. We will discuss this tonight. Hope we get leave,' smiled Ketan.

After an exuberant holiday, the routine and mundane life in office hit them hard. But both tried to let themselves get absorbed in it.

'Here comes the 'No more single guy,' Ketan's boss had patted his back and greeted him on his first day in office as a married man. His colleagues joined him soon and started talking about Malaysia. He could have spoken for hours, but in about an hour Ketan was on his seat working Laboriously. Amit's phone call came as a relief for Ketan.

Amit was married for a few years and also lived in Kolkata. His wife, Neha, was five months pregnant. Shiv lived in Bhubaneswar and was in a relationship with Shilpi, of Siliguri, for the past three years.

'Shiv and Shilpi are in town. Come over for dinner tonight along with Palak,' Amit almost ordered. Ketan was only too pleased to accept the invitation.

Minutes after the party began, Amit's neighbours could hear loud cheers from the house. But they were used to it now. They knew that when Shiv and Ketan came, the party could stretch up to at least 1 am. The friends were happy to see each other. They discussed the short honeymoon, Neha's pregnancy and the love affair of Shiv and Shilpi.

Ever since Neha announced her pregnancy, the couple had stayed at home. Her doctor had advised her not to travel in the first three months. When Amit said that he ached to travel, Shiv produced from his pockets six free air tickets to Bengaluru and back. His company had given them to him that day itself. The entire bunch was ecstatic seeing the tickets. They could take just a day's leave from office and slip out of town during the weekend. And Neha was comfortable now after the crucial three months of pregnancy were over.

'Let's go to Coorg in the Nilgiri Hills,' said Shiv. 'It's close to Bengaluru and no one had seen the place before.' They all wanted to see the coffee plantations and the thick vegetation of the Nilgiris. Coorg was connected to Bengaluru by an overnight bus. Immediately, all had their smart phones out and were looking for a decent hotel. They needed four rooms—one for each couple and another one to spend time together. The beautiful pictures posted online beckoned them. They zeroed-in on Night Queen, a small hotel which had only four rooms. All liked it as it would give them some privacy.

The next morning, Shiv called up the hotel. A lady picked up the phone. When Shiv said he wanted the fourth room to party, she gave a heavy discount on it. Then he reserved the bus. All six were jubilant on hearing this and started preparing for the weekend vacation.

Friday morning, they all boarded the flight and reached Bengaluru on time. After a short break, they took the bus and left for the hill station. Even before the day could break, they had reached Night Queen. This was actually a house with four rooms and a small lobby. It looked smaller than it appeared on the Internet, but was clean and well-maintained. Its ambience with the lovely green hills at the back made it look grand. A road, barely 500 metres from the hotel, connected the house to the main road.

As they entered, they were welcomed at the reception counter by a lady who would be around 65 years of age. She could speak both English and Hindi fluently. She said she had been waiting for them and gave them keys to the rooms. 'Please freshen up. I will send someone to take the breakfast order,' she said in her heavy voice.

In his own room, Amit found a comfortable corner for Neha and brought everything she would need within her reach. Neha fell asleep in an instant. He went for a shower, and was happy to feel the chill in the water, hardly ever felt in Kolkata. Seeing Neha comfortable, he left the room to discover the area.

The view from the hotel was, to say the least, breathtaking. The small lobby was made of glass. Through this, the hills looked lush and magnificent. The sky met the hills at a distance making the hills look blue—that's why the name, Nilgiri.

The lobby had a small door which led to a long, winding concrete pathway that connected the hotel to the owner's house. Tall bushes covered both sides of the pathway. Sitting inside the lobby one could clearly see the owner's house, but the entire pathway was not visible. The house was barely 25 metres away and at least 5 metres lower than the hotel.

At the top of the lobby door hung a lemon and some green chillies. The lemon had browned, but the chillies had still retained some colour.

Amit went out of the hotel through the pathway. The various shades of green, the fresh air and the tranquillity left him mesmerised. As he walked on the pathway with his hands deep inside his jacket pockets, he crossed a man who was going towards the hotel. When he stood there, he would see both the lobby as well as the house. However, at neither place could he see anyone. 'Perhaps, the family goes shopping at this hour,' he thought and walked on. Amit felt hypnotised by the beauty of Coorg and kept walking. He returned to the hotel when it was lunch time.

He was surprised that no one had missed him all this while. They hadn't because the others had been asleep all this while. But Amit was thankful that they had ordered lunch. He was famished.

Fried fish, home style chicken curry and rice—that was just the lunch he wanted. The food was served by the man Amit had seen at the pathway. His name was Jayan. He had thick, bushy eyebrows. For some reason, he would never look straight into anyone's eyes. 'How many people live here?' asked Shiv out of curiosity. 'Just me and my mother,' he said as he swayed his head from one side to the other. 'My mother has been here for more than 50 years now. We love being hospitable to tourists,' he added.

Shipli asked Jayan if there was any place around where they go and return before the evening. Jayan told them about a coffee plantation-turned-resort and a temple nearby. So after lunch all the tourists, except Neha, dressed and left for their little adventure. Neha was not sure if she could walk down the hills and preferred to rest at the hotel.

As she settled on her bed, she felt somewhat cold. She picked up the phone, called the old lady at the reception and told her that she needed a blanket. It did not take Jayan half a minute to reach her door with four blankets in hand. Neha was taken aback by Jayan's speed and asked him for some hot water as well. After about 30 minutes she saw through her window Jayan walking down the pavement with a bucket of water. But when the water came, it was the old lady carrying it. She was confused, and thinking about it dozed off in the bed.

When she woke up it was already dusk. The hot water was now freezing. She phoned Amit to ask about everybody's whereabouts. 'We are on the way, sweetie. We will reach the hotel in just 15 minutes,' he said.

When they reached, all gathered at the fourth extra room and had tea and cookies which were brought by Jayan. He took the dinner order and left. They discussed the places they had visited. Then Shiv brought out a bottle of whisky for the men and vodka for the ladies. He also ordered grape juice and ice.

As discussions became vibrant and high-pitched, Neha saw the lady come inside the lobby to switch on the lights. She had just about left the entrance and disappear when Neha saw Jayan appear at the pathway holding grape juice in one hand and ice in the other.

'Why are they never seen together?' Neha's thoughts made her shiver a little.

'You know, these places have ghosts,' she said aloud.

'When I was a little girl, I had gone to Kurseong, near Darjeeling, with my parents for a day. That night, all the staff at the hotel would go off to sleep at eight pm. It was pitch dark and quiet. I was so scared that night.'

Taking the lead, Shilpi began her story. 'In Siliguri

people say that voices beckon people in the middle of the night. These voices are usually of people one knows well—it could be an immediate family member or a close friend. The voices stupefy people, so much so that they start following the voice. They lure people towards a cliff. The next morning these people are found dead just below the cliff. Such stories are very common in the hills.'

'Oh! Ghost stories are common in Odisha too. There are people who can catch ghosts,' said Shiv. 'It is believed that when small children die they become evil and make a kind of buzzing noise. People who can hear the buzz can catch these ghosts.'

'But why on earth would anyone catch ghosts?' asked Amit.

'That's because these tiny ghosts steel cash and gold and take them away to some unknown place,' he said. Everyone laughed at Shiv's narrative.

Neha, who constantly had one eye on the lobby's door, saw Jayan near the house, coming towards the hotel. Within minutes, she saw the old lady open the lobby door. This had happened for the third time with Neha now. She persuaded Amit to call Jayan while the old lady was still in the room. At Amit's behest, the old lady went to the intercom to call Jayan. She picked it up and put it back immediately. 'The phone is down,' she said. 'I will have to go and call him.' Neha's legs started to shiver as she narrated the series of coincidences to everyone. All queued up at the door and watched the pathway. But no one came.

They returned to their seats and laughed at Neha's

suspicions. The discussion continued. It was Palak's turn now. 'When I was in high school, I used to go for maths tuitions on my bicycle. To reach the tutor's house I had to cross an unlit road. Both sides of the road had very tall trees. One night while I was returning, I felt my bicycle suddenly move rather slowly. I felt as if two people were sitting on the carrier of the bicycle. I was petrified. I did not look back and started to paddle fast. But my bike would not move faster. I paddled furiously. Soon I could see a light at the end of the road, and some people move about. I tried to apply brakes, but it was too tight. The rubber had jammed on the wheels of my bike. 'God! I was so relieved.'

'Remember college days, Shiv?' Amit said. 'You know Neha, when we were in the hostel, people told us not to put our feet down when the lights were switched off and no one was around. It was said that two long and strong arms pull you under the bed the moment you put your feet down.'

'And what would happen under the bed?' Neha asked.

'Well, the long arms would be of the seniors. They would cover themselves with a black bed sheet and wait under the bed,' Amit laughed.

'My parents used to say that when men die before marriage, they turn into demons. They sit on palm or coconut trees and their long feet touch the ground. Whenever someone passes by the trees, they see heads roll on the ground like leaves'. Added Palak.

By now, Neha was so scared she was perspiring despite the cold weather. Everyone had eaten the dinner that Jayan had served between the discussion. Neha, however, had been so engrossed listening to the horror stories that she had forgotten to eat. 'Let's all go and sleep,' she urged, rather scared to hear more such eerie stories. Amit was so drunk and tired that he slept the moment he fell on the bed. Neha kept looking outside the window at the pathway. She tried to remember a prayer—

In the dark and deep corners of mind,
There are thresholds and edges sharp,
Noises and this sea of screaming,
Distinct like the strings of harp!

When speech chokes itself in despair,
'Life loves to be taken by the lapel'
The ray of guidance in love and care,
Forms and God your scapel.

Yet again on lost dreams,
Hope keeps rolling now and new,
We do struggle with open eyes,
The womb of peace and you.

Take me through these edges sharp,
Give me the form I want to be.

'How come no one has seen the mother and the son together?' the thought kept nagging her. The house that could be seen through the window was pitch dark and absolutely silent. She stared hard at it trying to peer through its window. She saw nothing. Nothing happened. At 4 am she fell asleep.

Four years later, Neha's memories of the place were vivid. She would repeat her story to her friends. Amit partly believed her, and the rest ....

Twelve

MERCY KILLING—What does one say to a person who has an ever-smiling face, cracks jokes all the time, dresses immaculately and tries to keep everyone happy? The person prefers to keep quiet about things he does not know and gives an opinion only when asked for. He has a lot of free time and is always ready to go out for a walk, or a drink, and listen to your ranting. You can share your secrets with him and rest assured it will never reach anyone else's ears. That person is always there for you, and because of this, the natural thing to say to him is, 'I have lots to tell you.

'Wait. I will get back when I am free.'

It was December 24, 2005. Winters in Kolkata are cold, but not freezing. Mohit was still in bed when his father came to his room in the morning. He was very angry with Mohit and told him it was time he found a job for himself. Mohit understood that his parents had had a long discussion about him last night and his father's discourse was the result of the discussion. Mohit vaguely remembered last night. He had gone to attend a birthday party in the evening, got drunk and reached home very late. This was usual. He got home late and his parents' anger reached him the next morning.

Mohit had always been a below average student. He wanted to work, but did not quite know what to do. His parents were rich and had always met all his demands. The boy within him never grew up. He never quite understood why one needed to work. He never learnt to take life seriously. Born and bred in Kolkata, he had a large circle of friends. Some were from his school, others from college, and many more were his friends' friends.

A day before Christmas, he knew parties would go unrestrained today as well. Mohit had his breakfast and started calling up friends. 'Hey, wait. I'll call you back.' This was the usual response he would get from them. Today was nothing unusual. He knew they would call back. They usually had a lot to say to him. After all, he was the best listener.

Last night, Smita had called up to say she wanted to meet him. Mohit and Smita had been friends for long. She was leaving Kolkata because she had got a job as an underwriter in a life insurance company in Meerut. So, despite the hangover he pulled himself out of home at 11 am. They met at Golden Dragon in Park Street. It was a good but small restaurant for Chinese food. They ordered

Smita's favourite food—fried momos and chicken clear soup. Soon, Smita was spewing her apprehensions about the new office. After she finished, she did not have much to say. So she started talking about Mohit. 'You are still jobless, Mohit.'

'Yes, and I'm unmarried too. My father wants me to join his business. I hope after that he wouldn't wait to get me married,' he said.

Smita remembered the time when his father made him sit in his shop for a few days. 'I still cannot forget those few days,' she laughed. 'You would steal money so that we could have dosas, samosas and ice-cream. We have also had great parties with that money.'

While they were still reminiscing about the good old days, Mohit got a phone call from Sailen. As Smita paid the bill, she heard him talk. He was fixing another party. Sailen was also an old friend and it was his birthday today. The party was fixed at 6 pm at Oly Pub, a well-known bar-cum restaurant at Park Street.

Mohit had barely reached home when he got a phone call from Preeti, the most beautiful girl when they were in college. The tall and fair Punjabi girl worked in a media company that conducted events in The Park—a high-end hotel. Tonight, too, an event had been planned. She always called him when she needed a supply of marijuana. Mohit was too eager to attend the event, whatever it was. After 10 pm, The Park was the best hotel in Kolkata, and Preeti's events were fun and happening. Mohit had a crush on Preeti in college, but now she had a boyfriend.

Both Preeti and Sailen were very dear to him. So much so that talking to them made him forget his morning discussion with his father.

Oly Pub was throbbing when he got there at 6 pm. Sailen, Joshit, Suketu and Bappa were already two pegs down when Mohit entered the bar. Bappa was jobless but was working hard to find one. Joshit, Sailen and Suketu had stable jobs. Mohit was the only free bird.

'Remember December 31 night last year?' asked Sailen. 'Oh! What an awesome all-night party it was at Suketu's place. His house rocked with loud music and drinks. What fun we had. I remember the look Suketu's neighbour gave us the next morning when we were leaving.'

Alcohol flowed and the party went on. Mohit was the only one still conscious because he had not swalloued too many pegs like his friends had. He knew he had to meet Preeti. At 9 pm, Mohit got up and said, 'Guys, I will leave now. I have to meet someone.' After he left, Bappa and Sailen paid the bills.

Oly Pub and Park Hotel are close by, so Mohit was with Preeti within minutes of leaving his friends. Preeti began talking about boys she despised. Mohit gave them marijuana and soon the area around him was full of smoke. She began to talk about the woes of working as an event manager. 'Clients ask us to do such useless things, you know. Their demands are absolutely never-ending. And they never want to pay more,' her problems were endless. She had had a small fight with her boyfriend and was having problems at home.

Mohit's phone rang. It was Rahul. He knew why Rahul would have called at 11.30 at night. He usually got drunk by this time and wanted prostitutes. He would also insist on Mohit coming along. Mohit had never learnt to refuse anything to anyone. 'I am at The Park. Come and pick me up,' he lowered his voice as he said this. By now, Preeti had had her dose of marijuana and her sentences made absolutely no sense at all. He left her there and waited outside the hotel for Rahul.

The two travelled for almost 40 minutes and reached a hotel. As Rahul walked inside sheepishly, Mohit waited outside. His phone rang again. This time it was Priyanka. They had been neighbours since they were children. She had taken a flight to Kolkata from Mumbai. But there was no cab outside the airport. She wanted him to pick her up.

Mohit called up Rahul to tell him he wanted to leave. But his phone was switched off. So he left an SMS—'Need to meet someone urgently. Taking cab'.

It was almost 1 am, but it seemed Kolkata's traffic was growing by the minute. By the time he had reached the airport, Priyanka had called at least five times to check on his whereabouts. Each time he picked up the phone to tell her that he was on way. As he fiddled with his phone, he saw his father's six missed calls in the past two hours. He hadn't picked them up because of objectionable places he was in.

Mohit was happy to see Priyanka. She had lost weight and looked excited to be back. They hugged each other and entered the cab. Their homes were 9 kilometres away.

It should take not more than half an hour to get home. 'I will talk to Dad when I reach home,' he thought.

Five kilometres away, a road accident had occurred. Police persons had stopped all vehicles. The two had nothing to do but wait and talk. He listened to Priyanka's life in Mumbai, the traffic and the exorbitantly high house rents. But soon, she said she was tired and went off to sleep.

Vehicles had started to move now, but at an extraordinarily slow pace. His phone rang. It was Rahul. He put it on silent mode and did not pick it up. It rang again. This time, it was his father. 'If I pick up the phone and start talking, I will wake up Priyanka,' he thought. He looked at her in the dark. Her stole was too small to cover her bare shoulders. Her pretty complexion and full lips did not let him take his eyes off her. He had always liked Priyanka. 'What If I get married to Priyanka? After all, she is good looking and my parents know her parents.'

The cab screeched to a halt as the driver applied the brakes. A policeman wanted his vehicle documents. The driver quietly opened the door and went out with the documents. The light from a taxi nearby fell full on Priyanka's face. Mohit's stomach turned. He closed his eyes and started to think. He saw himself standing in front of his father. Standing beside him was a cheerful Priyanka in bridal dress.

A cold whiff woke him up from sleep. The cab was moving fast, as they had moved out of the problem area. 'We are reaching home,' he whispered into Priyanka's ears. But Priyanka was in deep sleep. He had to shake her to wake her up. It was 3 am. Both went to their own homes. It had been an eventful day for Mohit, but all that remained in his mind were the thoughts of Priyanka.

When he woke up the next morning, his father was standing at the foot of the bed as usual. The smile on his face confused Mohit. His father came and sat near him and said that he had found a job for him. He was to take care of the family's trading business in Sri Lanka along with his uncle. He had already booked the tickets, and would have to leave Kolkata at 10 am.

Mohit was happy at the prospect. He quickly picked up his phone to inform his friends about it. But Priyanka, Preeti, Rahul and Sailen did not pick up their phones. None of the others did either. Probably they had a hangover because of last night's escapades, or maybe they would call later....

Bundle of mistakes and misfortune,
In a moment then back to the moon,
What came across? What went wrong?
I always failed to realize soon...

Ah! My wits and concluding joke,
Laughter and giggles I always broke?...
Loud cheers and untamed nights,
Lost in people, then found in smoke!

LOST DISCUSSIONS

Where in years, what in noise,

I crafted myself in sonorous voice,

Who left alone, when I was effaced?

Why I was kept along with toys...

Times to come shall cheer me again,

Times when 'go' shall leave me alone...

Thirteen

AN ACCIDENT OF PERSPECTIVES—Aditya dragged himself out of bed that morning. His head ached and eyes felt groggy. He could barely keep his legs straight. Yet he picked up a towel and headed for the washroom for his bath. He had no option. He had an early appointment with the owners of a plastic bag manufacturing unit on the outskirts of Kolkata. His job was to assess promoters of the company and decide whether to lend them money or not.

Aditya worked for a finance company and handled its business in the eastern zone. He had lived all his life in Kolkata and loved the place. His father was a famous lawyer, so money flowed like a river inside the house. Almost every weekend, they would host parties. Invitees ranged from relatives, old school friends and office colleagues to music lovers. At parties, all that Aditya needed was someone who could relate to his intellectual and aesthetic needs.

Last night he had invited office colleagues and an old friend who loved to play the guitar. The guitarist arrived late, around 9 pm, but within minutes he was playing old Bengali and Hindi songs. In about an hour, the house seemed to be the venue for a live concert. Aditya loved music—good or bad made no difference. No matter who was playing, he would shake his head from side to side in admiration, and tap his thigh or the table along with the beat. Last night was one such, he remembered.

Dinner had been ordered from choicest restaurants. The best Lucknowi biryani and the kebabs in Kolkata had been served. Fish fillets fried crisp were prepared by the chief cook. Dessert was brought from the city's best sweet shop. But Aditya could not relish it. The sound of music gave him such a high that he forgot to have dinner. All that went inside his empty stomach was alcohol. He was not much of a drinker. The innumerable parties had taught him to drink within his limits. But last night was different. He had no control over himself when his friend started playing the guitar. He must have gulped down at least five pegs more than his usual.

Standing under the shower in the morning, songs still played at the back of his mind.

In rhythms and beats,

I followed my feet.

In men and women,

I found all omen.

Restless me just doing my job,
Guestless heart, relaxing a mob,
Unrest creeping on my eternity,
Questioning my own sagacity.

I crave to be a different one,
Aloof, agile like none.
My world has held me too close,
I am really sick of daily blows.

Will reap a seed I didn't sow,
Will do something I don't know.

Breakfast was laid, but he had no appetite. When Bhola, the driver, called on his phone that the company's car had arrived, he rushed out leaving the sandwiches uneaten on the table. As soon as he entered the car, the smell of cheap perfume and sweat overpowered him. It was for this reason that he got his own Volkswagen cleaned every day before he left home. But today it was the company's car, so he could not complain.

He had to pick up Saurabh Sethi, his subordinate, on the way. Aditya admired him for his excellent singing skills. The two hit it off well and whenever they went on long distance tours, they would sit in the evening for a couple of drinks and singing sessions. There might be another session this evening, thought Saurabh cheerfully as he got inside the car along with the documents required for the meeting.

The unpleasant odour inside the car made Aditya extremely uncomfortable. Kolkata's sultry weather added to the discomfort. But he refused to pull down the windows. The dust outside would increase his allergy. He chose bad odour over allergy. Last night's hangover made him reach for his bottle of water every five minutes. He needed it to cool his bowels.

The songs played last night still reverberated in the minds of both. Saurabh started singing one and then two discussed it threadbare—its singer, lyricist, its beat—almost everything. Then they started talking about personal finance. The topics changed by every minute—from politics to sports, to the millionaires in the city.

The journey seemed smooth. As per schedule, they had left the city by 10 am and hit Kona Expressway, the road which connects the city with the industrial area. When they reached the factory unit, the promoters were ready to welcome them. They showed their unit. But they were far too garrulous in explaining the performance of their unit than Aditya could suffer. They offered them tea and snacks which Saurabh accepted twice, much to Aditya's chagrin. His hangover was bothering him, but the meeting continued. It was almost 2 pm when the meeting got over. The lenders had decided to lend the money.

Aditya's empty stomach had started to growl. He finished the conversation rather abruptly and ran inside the car. Saurabh followed. He instructed Bhola to take the car to their usual dhaba. The food here was quite good. He could almost see the dhaba on the right hand side of the road.

Aditya asked Bhola to stop the car on the left to avoid taking the U-turn. Just as it stopped, he turned to pick up the water bottle and at the same time opened the car door towards the highway. Before he could step out, the screech of a braking motorbike, the loud horn of a truck and the squeal of a man in pain left everyone around stunned. The biker, who was driving right behind the car, hit the edge of its door, lost control and swooped underneath a slow moving truck. The truck drove for about five metres before stopping, taking the bike along with him. Aditya was aghast as he watched this from inside the car.

Completely unhinged, he stepped out of the car as the biker yelled in pain and struggled to come out from under the rear wheels of the truck. Aditya ran to help the biker come out and gave him his shoulder. The biker was up on his feet and was trying to walk somehow. He had sustained deep cuts on the thighs and arms. He looked very angry and went up to the truck driver to shout at him despite the pain. Aditya was taken aback by his sudden agility. But he was more mortified by the accident, for which he blamed himself. 'I could have killed someone because of my carelessness,' he said to himself.

By now, Saurabh appeared beside him and was holding his shoulders as if reassuring that he would stand by him in any hour of crisis. The small physical gesture helped Aditya breathe easy. Together they tried to bring out the bike from under the truck. It was completely broken from the front and the front wheel was smashed. Worse, the dismantled parts had got stuck to the truck.

The biker and the truck driver had started a heated argument and blamed each other for the accident. Aditya went to the truck driver and asked him to move his vehicle so that the bike could be moved out. The truck driver looked at Aditya from head to toe. His expensive suit and the many gadgets hanging on him gave away his social stature. Without saying a word, he climbed on to his seat, started the truck and flew the vehicle. In a blink, the truck was out of sight.

The biker had not stopped shouting at him. People who had gathered to watch the show accused the truck driver of reckless driving. 'Either the truck's driver or its owner should pay the biker for the damages,' said one. 'Repair and medical bills will cost a bomb'.

Aditya placed the bike on one side of the road and took the biker to a small shop on the roadside. They sat and together drank many glasses of water that the shopkeeper had brought for them. The biker told him he was a small-time worker at a factory nearby. Aditya folded his hands in front of the biker and started to apologise profusely. He told him that they would take him to a hospital for first-aid. But his words seemed to be falling on deaf ears. He was looking at his wounds and seemed more annoyed with the truck driver.

By now, the biker's friend had reached the accident site. They started talking to each other in a very low tone. To the utter surprise of Aditya and Saurabh, the injured and his friend thought it was more important to take the bike to the garage than go to a hospital. 'Please have your lunch,' they told Aditya and Saurabh, and then arranged for a vehicle that could take the damaged bike to the garage.

Aditya found it impossible to eat. It disturbed him that at a time when someone had escaped death by the whiskers, people were interested in talking about cash, cops and crime. He left his lunch that had already reached his table, and went back to the biker. He started to apologise once again and asked him to go to a hospital.

It was almost 4 pm. As Saurabh made phone calls to call off the 4.30 meeting, the biker's friend came up to him. 'Please pay Rs 5,000 and we will take him to a hospital.' Aditya was taken aback at the small demand. For someone who earned Rs 2 lakh per month, Rs 5,000 was a pittance. 'I will pay right now. Please take your friend to a hospital. The bike can be sent to the garage by someone else. Keep my business card in case you need any help.'

Aditya went the car, took out money from his wallet and paid. He then took the biker's phone number. He wanted to call him up at night to know that all was well.

He then paid to the dhaba for the uneaten food and left. The biker and his friend still sat near the shop.

With the evening meeting cancelled, Saurabh and Aditya decided to spend the evening at a typical countryside bar which served cheap beer and fried chicken. Instead of music, the topic of discussion was the accident. 'You looked so disturbed. I could not even tell you anything because there were so many people around,' said Saurabh. 'I wonder what kind of a person that man was! A fraction of a second after the accident, he was yelling at the truck driver asking for compensation amount'.

'Well, I'm still unnerved,' said Aditya.

'You know, the biker was looking at you suspiciously because you had got busy pulling the bike from under the truck. He wanted it to remain there so that a hefty sum could be extracted from the truck's driver or owner,' said Saurabh.

'This poor biker must have a family. Was it only money that he wanted? Did he have other things in his mind?' wondered Aditya.

It was 6.30 pm now. Both had already finished three glasses of beer each. The topic of discussion had not changed. Just then Aditya saw the biker and his friend walk into the bar. As they sat down, he saw the biker had a bandage on his left arm and was limping. He had changed his shirt. The smell of cheap perfume and sweat inside the bar once again made Aditya uncomfortable.

Fourteen

LABIAL—Rohit and Sneha were good friends. Both belonged to Sikar, a small town some 100 kilometres from Jaipur. Both had studied in the same school since childhood and knew each other for years. Rohit left the school when his parents decided that he should do high-schooling from Delhi. Yet, the friends stayed in touch. There was nothing that the two did not know about each other. Their families were friends, too. There was nothing that could be called love between each other. But that was only till Munna joined.

Rohit was still in the school in Sikar when Munna had joined. They became friends. Through Rohit, Munna met Sneha and immediately fell in love with her. He told Rohit how much he adored her. He would scribble sweet nothings on chits of paper and send them to Sneha through Rohit. Rohit would run to Sneha and together they would laugh out loud reading the messages.

When Rohit joined college in Delhi, his friend helped him concentrate on studies. But he would wait impatiently for weekends and rush home. At the hostel, all the boys would have their own love stories to narrate. And then, Rohit would think of Sneha's black, bold eyes, her long neck and vibrant face. He thought he liked Sneha much more than he knew it himself.

This time something pulled him towards home. He took leave from college despite exams being just round the corner. When he reached Sikar, Munna put pressure on him to go to Sneha's house to meet her.

Sneha had a brother and a sister. Her father had retired from a state government department.

That day, when Munna asked Rohit to take him to Sneha's place in the evening, he could not refuse. But Rohit felt extremely uncomfortable there today. When they entered Sneha's house, his parents gave Rohit a strange smile. Their siblings looked suspiciously at him. And why had Sneha dressed up? He could not understand. She looked lovely that day. Rohit felt attracted towards her, but refrained from taking any step when he saw Munna's eyes adoringly fixed on her. 'May be Sneha likes Munna too,' he thought.

Munna barely said anything throughout tea. He then mumbled that he had to meet someone and left early. Sneha laughed at his nervousness. After tea, her parents went inside the house and her brother and sister got busy with their work.

Sneha and Rohit were left alone. This was the place where the two had spent so much time together playing board games, studying and at times just chatting; but today seemed different.

'These days you don't talk much to me,' giggled Sneha, 'What's the problem? Are you scared of talking to a young girl?'

Her words made Rohit even more uncomfortable. He felt breathless and got up to go towards the window. But Sneha pulled his hand and admitted that she loved him.

Rohit was terrified when he heard this. Sneha's parents knew his parents so well. What would happen if they got to know? His legs shook when he thought of all his fears—the fear of people getting to know of their love, fear of touching a girl, fear of kissing her on the lips...

His cheeks and ears felt as if they were in flames. He rushed out of the house saying he would call her the next morning.

A tingling sensation kept Rohit awake that entire night. But the morning seemed more beautiful today. After many years, he was able to admire the beauty of nature. The trees looked greener, the birds sang melodiously today, and even his mother's boring breakfast seemed delicious. But he was unable to eat. His stomach was churning with anxiety. He had promised Sneha that he would call in the morning. He could not do so from home. His mother would have surely heard him. He decided to go to the telephone booth, which was barely half a kilometre from his house.

When he got there, it took him another half an hour to muster courage to dial Sneha's phone number. Within two rings, Sneha picked up the phone. 'Was she waiting for his call?' Rohit wondered, but could barely speak. He was a bundle of nerves and heart beats. He felt as if his tongue had tied into a knot.

'Rohit?' asked Sneha.

After taking in a couple of long breaths, Rohit said, 'Yes. Can we meet today for a movie? I have to return to Delhi tonight.'

'OK. Which theatre? And what time?'

'The 5 o'clock show,' he said and quickly put the receiver down.

He had told his parents that he would take the train to Delhi at 12.30 pm. He felt strange from within and wanted to hide somewhere. He took out money from his pocket and went to buy movie tickets for the evening. But the man at the counter told him he would get them only after 4.30 pm. He went to a hotel and ordered *Daal Makhni* and *Tandoor rotis* that he loved so much. But he did not relish it today and left it half eaten. He gulped down two bottles of water.

The clock kept ticking. He felt this was the slowest day in his life. At 4.30 pm sharp, he was at the movie hall's counter and had bought two tickets. He then went and bought himself another bottle of water. Just then, he saw Sneha walking towards him. She wore a beautiful red T-shirt and a pair of light blue jeans. She looked fresh and excited. The heat had done nothing to harm her. He hadn't seen her look so beautiful ever. He felt small and weak. He was so scared that he wanted to take an about-turn and run home. But he mustered courage and walked up to her. His legs shook again, but his face had a pleasant and confident smile.

'You didn't even tell me which theatre I was to come...I just guessed it would be this one,' she laughed.

'Why is she laughing so loudly? What if someone who knows us sees us together?' Rohit was perspiring hard now. He looked around and checked on each one around him. Then he happily slipped his hand into hers and walked inside the movie hall.

The air-conditioner inside made Rohit comfortable, and he started to feel normal again. It was a relief that none of the seats around them were occupied.

When the lights turned off for the show to begin, Rohit finished the bottle of water that he had just bought.

Sneha got engrossed in the movie, while Rohit was trying to overcome a challenge within. He wanted to tell her that he felt like a grown-up man. He did not know if he loved her, but he definitely wanted to kiss her.

It happened within seconds. He pulled her face towards him and kissed her long. The next moment, both moved away from each other. The movie ran, but they weren't watching it any more. Within half an hour, both left the hall.

Rohit jumped into the bus for Delhi and took the last seat. He was no longer perspiring. He closed his eyes and relived those precious moments of happiness with Sneha. Or, were they the moments that sent one on guilt trips? He was not sure. He went into deep sleep, as this song played in the bus—

On promises and commitments,
On difficulties yet reasonably true,
One keeps the expectation high,
Yet there is everything blue.

Like an ocean becomes the sky,
This verity was never my.

What dies are relationships,
Not a person, not a soul,
This wanton breach, this hullabaloo
Yet life is, and it has to roll.

Something that ends is an episode.
Begins now a new tale,
How things would culminate
Make my face, my heart pale.

Rohit reached the hostel at 10.30 pm. Here, he had made two friends—Sushil and DK. Sushil was a good boy from Jaipur. All parents would give his example while trying to correct their own sons. He was excellent in academics as well as in sports. He respected his seniors, parents and teachers. Students envied him and wanted to follow him.

DK, on the other hand, was least interested in studies. He lived in the hostel despite his parents staying in Delhi. This was an arrangement to ward off the feeling of loneliness he had at home. He rarely attended classes and had failed a year. He had learnt to smoke and drink. He wore high fashion clothes and bought new gadgets every now and then. He would manage to escape the warden's eyes and return late to the hostel. And then he would wake up everyone and share long stories of his escapades.

When Rohit reached the hostel, Sushil was studying.

'But weren't you supposed to come tomorrow?' Sushil asked surprised to see him a day earlier than promised.

'I thought I would miss that important physics class.'

'Hmm...Did you meet Munna and Sneha? I know you have. It's written all over your face. Come out with it. Tell me what happened,' he said closing his books and lying down.

Rohit had changed and was inside his bed, too, by now. But his face was long, as if ashamed of himself.

'I took Sneha to a movie today.'

'Oh, which movie?'

'I don't remember!'

'So what happened there? Wasn't Munna around? Did you have a fight?'

'No. I kissed Sneha. Munnna was not there.'

'You kissed Sneha? Why? I mean...'

There was a long silence. And then Sushil started

again, 'You do not love her. So you should not have kissed her. Even if you do love her, will you marry her? What will Munna think of you? It's really bad. You should be ashamed of yourself.'

'I think I love her, Sushil. Well, at least I feel attracted towards her. When I went home this time, my eyes kept glued to her throughout. I felt I should do something for her...may be take her out of Jaipur.'

'Are you serious, Rohit? You have not even completed college. You are not sure how well you will do this year in the final exams. You belong to a family that is waiting for you to finish studies and start earning. And you are thinking of taking Sneha out of Jaipur? What do you want to do? Bring her to this hostel? You have gone crazy. You are spending too much time with fools. This is what it has done to your basic understanding of life.'

'I just thought that she was expecting something from me. I did whatever I could. I may marry her later...who knows.'

'Well, what I know is that if you fail in your exam you will have to return to Jaipur and take up a very small job. Getting married, Huh!' Sushil finished sarcastically.

The door flung open and DK entered, reeking of perfume, 'Who is getting married?'

It was almost 12 at night. He sat on his bed and carelessly threw his expensive pair shoes on one side. Before he got a response to his query, he started on his own story.

'Guys, today I was in a cab. When I was returning from Gurgaon, I saw a girl waiting for a lift. You know, she works at a call centre,' said DK.

Sushil covered his head with the bed sheet. He knew what was coming. He was never interested in DK's narratives. Rohit got up and sat on DK's bed to listen to his story. Something under the bed sheet poked him, but he was so eager to hear DK's story that he disregarded it.

'You know, when people see me they fall for me in an instant. I got down from the cab and offered her a lift, and the next moment she was inside the cab,' DK smiled. His was more about himself than the girl. Soon, Rohit got disinterested and told him about his own shameful escapade with Sneha.

DK laughed hard listening to Rohit's story. He congratulated Rohit and wondered why he was ashamed. Something was still poking him from under the bed sheet. He got up and went back to his bed. Soon, he could hear DK snoring. Suddenly DK screamed, pulled out something from inside the bed and threw it on Rohit. 'This is your yardstick. I used it yesterday.'

He picked it up and started to think. What Sushil found so grossly wrong was absolutely all right for DK. So what, actually, is correct? He realized that everyone has their own yardsticks. They can measure things, feelings, people, right and wrong the way they want to.

He thought of Sneha, smiled, and was asleep within a minute, still holding his yardstick.